红厅论坛
读懂中国共产党二十大

Hong Ting Forum
Understanding the 20th CPC National Congress

（中英双语）

(Chinese-English)

中央党史和文献研究院科研规划部、新华社研究院 编

Compiled by the Research and Planning Department of the Institute of
Party History and Literature of the CPC Central Committee and Xinhua Institute

中央党史和文献研究院第六研究部、新华社研究院 译

Translated by the Sixth Research Department of the Institute of
Party History and Literature of the CPC Central Committee and Xinhua Institute

图书在版编目（CIP）数据

红厅论坛：读懂中国共产党二十大：汉、英／
中央党史和文献研究院科研规划部，新华社研究院编；
中央党史和文献研究院第六研究部，新华社研究院译. —
北京：中央编译出版社，2023.11
　ISBN 978-7-5117-4380-0

Ⅰ.①红… Ⅱ.①中… ②新… ③中… Ⅲ.①中共
二十大（2022）-文集-汉、英 Ⅳ.①D220-53
中国国家版本馆 CIP 数据核字（2023）第 203520 号

红厅论坛：读懂中国共产党二十大（中英双语）

责任编辑	李小燕　付　瑾
责任印制	李　颖
出版发行	中央编译出版社
网　　址	www.cctpcm.com
地　　址	北京市海淀区北四环西路 69 号（100080）
电　　话	（010）55627391（总编室）　　（010）55627340（编辑室）
	（010）55627320（发行部）　　（010）55627377（新技术部）
经　　销	全国新华书店
印　　刷	北京文昌阁彩色印刷有限责任公司
开　　本	710 毫米×1000 毫米　1/16
字　　数	143 千字
印　　张	10
版　　次	2023 年 11 月第 1 版
印　　次	2023 年 11 月第 1 次印刷
定　　价	68.00 元

新浪微博：@中央编译出版社　　　微　信：中央编译出版社（ID: cctphome）
淘宝店铺：中央编译出版社直销店（http://shop108367160.taobao.com）　（010）55627331

本社常年法律顾问：北京市吴栾赵阎律师事务所律师　　闫军　梁勤
凡有印装质量问题，本社负责调换，电话：（010）55627320

前　言

2022年11月2日，中国共产党第二十次全国代表大会闭幕不久，中共中央党史和文献研究院与新华通讯社在中国共产党历史展览馆联合主办"红厅论坛：读懂中国共产党二十大"国际研讨会。论坛面向全球阐释宣介中国共产党二十大报告中的新概念、新范畴、新表述，围绕"关键在党""中国式现代化""中华优秀传统文化"等议题展开深入研讨。两家单位的领导和专家、参与大会文件翻译的外国专家代表、参与大会报道的编辑记者代表、国外智库学者代表等共19人在论坛上发言，中外智库和媒体嘉宾180余人参加论坛。论坛召开后，国内外媒体和学界反响热烈，论坛专家的发言观点被多家国外媒体转载刊发，论坛的国际影响力不断扩大。

为进一步满足国际社会和国内各界了解中国共产党最新理论和实践成果的需求，更好展示"红厅论坛：读懂中国共产党二十大"国际研讨会上的国内外智库专家观点，特将19位领导和专家发言的中文和英文文稿编辑成册出版。

"红厅论坛：读懂中国共产党二十大"国际研讨会论文集的编辑出版得到了中共中央党史和文献研究院与新华通讯社两家单位领导的关心和指导。中共中央党史和文献研究院科研规划部与新华社研究院承担了论文集的编辑工作，中共中央党史和文献研究院第六研究部与新华社研究院承担了论文集的翻译工作。

中共中央党史和文献研究院参与编辑工作的有张鹏、李琦、刘敏茹、范为、田江锋、桑田、周冰若，参与翻译工作的有刘亮、姜睿、孙显辉、朱艳辉、宋虹、俞婷宁、孙宁、钟晓辉、李煜敏、贾世璇、崔瑞、朱曼青、周冰若、肖恩、福佩吉。

新华通讯社参与编辑和翻译工作的有刘刚、崔峰、刘华、孙萍、刘阳、李桃、杜洋、赵熠煊。

中央编译出版社对论文的集结出版给与了大力支持，在此一并表示感谢。

编者

2023 年 4 月

Preface

On November 2, 2022, shortly after the 20th National Congress of the Communist Party of China came to a close, the Institute of Party History and Literature of the CPC Central Committee and Xinhua News Agency jointly hosted an international symposium at the Museum of the Communist Party of China in Beijing. The symposium was titled "Hong Ting Forum: Understanding the 20th CPC National Congress." The forum aimed to interpret the new concepts, frameworks, and formulations set forth in the report to the CPC's 20th National Congress for an international audience, with participants conducting in-depth discussions on topics such as "Key Role of the CPC," "Chinese Modernization," and "China's Fine Traditional Culture." Nineteen participants delivered speeches during the meeting. Among the speakers were leaders and experts from the Institute and Xinhua News Agency, foreign experts who participated in the translation of the official documents of the 20th National Congress, editors and reporters who covered the Congress, and scholars from overseas think tanks. Over 180 guests from Chinese and international think tanks and media organizations were also in attendance. After it closed, the forum received a positive response from both Chinese and foreign media and academia. With the publication of the views of experts in attendance by many foreign media outlets, the forum's international influence was further extended.

To help the international community and various sectors in China further understand the CPC's latest theories and practical achievements and better showcase the views of Chinese and foreign think-tank experts who attended the forum, we have compiled the Chinese and English editions of the 19 speeches delivered by attending leaders and experts into a single collection for publication.

Leaders from both the Institute of Party History and Literature of the CPC Central Committee and Xinhua News Agency closely followed and guided the work of editing and publishing this collection. Editing was carried out by the Institute's Research and Planning Department in conjunction with the Xinhua Institute, while the translation work was completed by the Institute's Sixth Research Department along with the Xinhua Institute.

The following personnel from the Institute of Party History and Literature of the CPC Central Committee participated in the editing work: Zhang Peng, Li Qi, Liu Minru, Fan Wei, Tian Jiangfeng, Sang Tian, and Zhou Bingruo. The following individuals from the Institute participated in the translation work: Liu Liang, Jiang Rui, Sun Xianhui, Zhu Yanhui, Song Hong, Yu Tingning, Sun Ning, Zhong Xiaohui, Li Yumin, Jia Shixuan, Cui Rui, Zhu Manqing, Zhou Bingruo, Sean Slattery, and Peggy Cantave Fuyet.

The members of Xinhua News Agency who participated in the editing and translation work were as follows: Liu Gang, Cui Feng, Liu Hua, Sun Ping, Liu Yang, Li Tao, Du Yang, and Zhao Yixuan.

We would like to take this opportunity to express our gratitude to the Central Compilation and Translation Press, which provided strong support for the publication of this collection.

Editorial Team
April 2023

目 录

在"红厅论坛:读懂中国共产党二十大"主题
　　研讨会开幕式上的致辞 ………………………… 曲青山　1
在"红厅论坛:读懂中国共产党二十大"主题
　　研讨会上的致辞 ………………………………… 傅　华　5

关键在党 ……………………………………………………… 9
办好中国的事,关键在党 ………………………… 黄一兵　11
全面建设社会主义现代化国家关键在中国共产党
　　——理解中共二十大精神的一个重要视角 …… 张贺福　15
跟着中国共产党走,是人民的选择、历史的必然 ……… 张旭东　18
解读中共二十大:中国共产党的关键作用 ……… 苏傲古　21
中国式现代化与共同富裕 ………………………… 肖　恩　23
中国共产党在各个领域的关键作用 …… 舍拉迪尔·巴克特古洛夫　26

中国式现代化 ………………………………………………… 29
以中国式现代化全面推进中华民族伟大复兴 …… 赵　承　31
"中国式现代化"概念及翻译 …………………… 张士义　35
民族复兴和人民幸福:理解"中国式现代化"的
　　两把钥匙 ………………………………………… 杨明伟　37

— 1 —

以公平公正为核心：中国式现代化的前进方向 ………… 马丁·雅克 40
中国式现代化为世界带来启发 ………………………… 福佩吉 42
中国式现代化和全球合作 ……………………… 哈利德·阿克拉姆 45

中华优秀传统文化 …………………………………………… 47

关于中华优秀传统文化 ………………………………… 王均伟 49
大力弘扬中华优秀传统文化 不断推进马克思主义
　　中国化时代化 ………………………………………… 刘荣刚 53
传承中华优秀传统文化 铸牢中华民族共同体意识 ………… 傅 琰 56
二十大报告中的中华优秀传统文化 ……………………… 安 吉 59
中共二十大的文化与发展 ……………… 德拉加娜·米特罗维奇 61

Contents

Speech at the Opening Ceremony of the "Hong Ting Forum: Understanding the 20th CPC National Congress" Seminar ·· Qu Qingshan 63

Speech at "Hong Ting Forum: Understanding the 20th CPC National Congress" Seminar ·· Fu Hua 69

The Key Role of the Communist Party of China ·························· 75

CPC Is Pivotal to China's Success ····························· Huang Yibing 77

Pivotal Role of the CPC in Building China into a Modern Socialist Country in All Respects
　—An Important Perspective to Understand the Guiding
　　Principles of the 20th CPC National Congress ··············· Zhang Hefu 84

History and the People Have Chosen the Communist Party of China ·· Zhang Xudong 88

An Interpretation of the 20th CPC National Congress: The Key Role of the CPC ····························· Augusto Soto 92

Chinese Modernization and Common Prosperity ············ Sean Slattery 95

The Key Role of the Communist Party of China in Various Fields ··································· Sheradil Baktygulov 98

| Hong Ting Forum: Understanding the 20th CPC National Congress

Chinese Modernization ········· 103

To Advance the Rejuvenation of the Chinese Nation
on All Fronts Through a Chinese Path to Modernization ······ Zhao Cheng   105

Chinese Modernization: Concept and Translation ············ Zhang Shiyi   111

National Rejuvenation and People's Wellbeing: Two
Keys to Understanding Chinese Modernization ············ Yang Mingwei   114

Chinese Modernization Includes the Idea of a More
Equitable and Fairer Society ························ Martin Jacques   118

The Chinese Modernization Offers New Options and
Opportunities to the World ···················· Peggy Cantave Fuyet   121

China's Modernization and Global Cooperation ······ Khalid Taimur Akram   124

China's Fine Traditional Culture ········· 127

On China's Fine Traditional Culture ···················· Wang Junwei   129

Vigorously Promoting Fine Traditional Chinese Culture
and Continuously Adapting Marxism to the Chinese
Context and the Needs of Our Times ···················· Liu Ronggang   135

Carrying Forward Fine Traditional Chinese Culture and
Fostering a Strong Sense of Community for the Chinese
Nation ·· Fu Yan   139

Traditional Chinese Culture Highlighted in the Report
to the 20th National Congress of the Communist Party
of China ·· K. Angelina   143

The 20th CPC National Congress: Culture and
Development ································· Dragana Mitrovic   146

在"红厅论坛:读懂中国共产党二十大"主题研讨会开幕式上的致辞

曲青山

中央党史和文献研究院院长
中央党史和文献研究院国家高端智库理事会理事长

尊敬的各位代表,
各位嘉宾,
女士们,先生们,朋友们:

大家下午好!今天,来自世界近80个国家的驻华使节代表、智库专家和媒体记者,来自中国的中央有关部门、国家高端智库机构和中央媒体的代表,共聚一堂,以现场出席或视频连线的方式参加首届红厅论坛,围绕中共二十大提出的新概念、新范畴、新表述深入探讨,相互交流。首先,我谨代表中共中央党史和文献研究院,对各位嘉宾的到来表示热烈欢迎!

十天前,中国共产党第二十次全国代表大会胜利闭幕。这次大会,是在中国共产党和中国各族人民迈上全面建设社会主义现代化国家新征程、向第二个百年奋斗目标进军的关键时刻召开的一次十分重要的大会。习近平总书记在大会上所作的报告,全面回顾总结过去五年的工作和新时代十年的伟大变革,明确了新时代新征程中国共产党的使命任务,科学擘画了未来五年乃至更长时期党和国家事业的发展目标和大政方针。中共中央党史和文献研究院与新华社,作为两家中国国家高端智库,以"读懂中国共产党二十大"为主题,共同举办此次论坛,为国际社会及时深入了解我们党的理念和主张,提供了一个交流沟通的有力平台。

今天借此机会，我结合对中共二十大精神的学习领会，谈几点认识和思考，与大家交流分享。

第一，中国共产党是全面推进中华民族伟大复兴的坚强领导力量。中共二十大报告指出："全面建设社会主义现代化国家、全面推进中华民族伟大复兴，关键在党。"

中国共产党是为中国人民谋幸福，为中华民族谋复兴的党，也是为人类谋进步，为世界谋大同的党。一百多年来，中国共产党不忘初心，牢记使命，砥砺前行。特别是新时代十年来，在以习近平同志为核心的党中央坚强领导下，我们党坚定而自觉地践行初心使命，带领中华民族推进从站起来、富起来到强起来的伟大飞跃。

一代又一代中国共产党人始终坚持以人民为中心，始终坚持人民至上，始终为把人民对美好生活的向往变为现实而不懈奋斗。我们深知，人民真正享受到美好生活，就会更加广泛地、发自内心地坚定支持我们的党。亿万人民的衷心爱戴和支持，是我们党长期执政的最大底气。

当然，作为一个长期执政的大国大党，我们党必然面对着复杂多变的环境，必须时刻准备迎接更加严峻的风险挑战。党必须不断进行自我革命，不断加强自身建设，提高执政能力，保持自身的先进性纯洁性，只有这样，才能更好地团结带领中国人民担负起自己的历史使命。

第二，以中国式现代化全面推进中华民族伟大复兴，是新时代新征程中国共产党的使命任务。中共二十大报告提出，"从现在起，中国共产党的中心任务就是团结带领全国各族人民全面建成社会主义现代化强国、实现第二个百年奋斗目标，以中国式现代化全面推进中华民族伟大复兴。"

实现现代化，是世界各国人民共同的追求。经过新中国成立特别是改革开放以来长期探索和实践，经过中共十八大以来在理论和实践上的创新突破，我们党成功推进和拓展了中国式现代化。中国式现代化，既有各国现代化的共同特征，更有基于自己国情的中国特色，这就是：人口规模巨大，全体人民共同富裕，物质文明和精神文明相协调，人与自然和谐共生，走和平发展道路。

这里，我想特别强调中国式现代化所坚持的和平发展道路。中国绝不会走一些国家通过战争、殖民、掠夺等方式实现现代化的老路，而是坚持国家间相互尊重、平等合作、共同发展。我们愿与世界各国一道，弘扬和平、发展、公平、正义、民主、自由的全人类共同价值，愿以中国的新发展为世界提供新机遇，不断推动构建人类命运共同体，创造人类文明新形态，为解决人类共同面临的现代化路径问题，提供积极有益的中国智慧、中国方案、中国力量！

第三，中华优秀传统文化是中国共产党全面推进中华民族伟大复兴的深厚精神支撑。中共二十大报告指出：中华优秀传统文化源远流长、博大精深，是中华文明的智慧结晶，同科学社会主义价值观主张具有高度契合性。

中华民族生生不息绵延发展、饱受挫折又不断浴火重生，离不开中华文化的丰厚滋养和强劲支撑。中华优秀传统文化，是中华民族的根和魂，也是中国共产党坚定历史自信和文化自信的深厚渊源，是我们在世界文化激荡中站稳脚跟的基石。

中国共产党是在中华大地上孕育和成长起来的政党，天然地继承了中华文化的优秀基因，中国共产党人始终是中华优秀传统文化的忠实继承者和弘扬者。大道之行、天下为公的大同理想，民为邦本、政在养民的民本思想，亲仁善邻、协和万邦的外交之道，以和为贵、好战必亡的和平理念等等，中国优秀传统政治文化和治国智慧，为我们党治国理政成功实践提供了深厚历史底蕴、重要文化滋养和磅礴精神力量。

中华文化同各国多彩文化具有共通性，通过不同文明交流互鉴、不同文化相互融合，中华优秀传统文化一定能够与各国人民创造的优秀文化一道，为人类提供正确精神指引。

女士们、先生们、朋友们！

当前，世界百年未有之大变局加速演进。面对复杂的国际环境，世界各国需要进一步加强交流合作，共同推动构建人类命运共同体，共同应对各种风险挑战。

中共中央党史和文献研究院承担着构建党的理论研究综合体系，打造党的历史和理论研究高端平台,建设党中央可靠的文献库、思想库、智囊团的重要职责。新华社是中国国家通讯社,也是世界级通讯社。未来,两家高端智库将携手合作,通过智库研讨形式,为国际社会深入了解中国共产党历史和理论的新概念、新范畴和新表述,持续提供对话平台。我们愿与智库专家和媒体朋友一道,进一步加强交流互鉴,让世界更好地了解中国、了解中国人民、了解中国共产党。

希望大家围绕此次论坛的主题深入探讨交流,启迪智慧,激荡思想,凝聚共识。最后,预祝本次论坛圆满成功!

谢谢大家。

在"红厅论坛:读懂中国共产党二十大"主题研讨会上的致辞

傅 华

新华通讯社社长
新华社国家高端智库学术委员会主任

尊敬的曲青山院长,

各位嘉宾,

女士们,先生们,朋友们:

大家好,很高兴与大家相聚在中国共产党历史展览馆。在举世瞩目的中共二十大胜利闭幕不久,我们在这座百年党史殿堂中举办"红厅论坛:读懂中国共产党二十大"主题研讨活动,具有特殊的意义。

中国共产党第二十次全国代表大会,是在全党全国各族人民迈上全面建设社会主义现代化国家新征程、向第二个百年奋斗目标进军的关键时刻召开的一次十分重要的大会。习近平总书记的报告,是中国共产党团结带领全国各族人民夺取中国特色社会主义新胜利的政治宣言和行动纲领,也为世界读懂中国提供了思想窗口和精神标识。

连日来,中共二十大受到国际社会高度关注。在新华社记者采访过程中,我们听到许多国际人士的声音。他们表示,中共二十大具有重要里程碑意义,不仅对中国产生深远影响,也为世界各国携手应对挑战、实现共同发展注入动力;中国共产党在过去一百年开创了中国发展的新道路,中共二十大必将深刻影响中国的未来发展,也期待中国共产党在新的历史起点上为世界作出更大贡献。这些心声反映了国际社会对中共二十大的高度评价，也反映了国际社会对了解中共二十大精神的愿望和需求。

为向世界更好地介绍中共二十大，回应国际社会关切，新华社与中央党史和文献研究院联合主办了这次论坛，设立"关键在党""中国式现代化""中华优秀传统文化"三个议题，旨在通过深入研讨交流，展示中共二十大的重要成果和重大意义，推动国际社会进一步了解中国共产党的执政理念和治国方略。

——**读懂中共二十大，首先要读懂中国共产党创新理论的真理力量**。中国共产党为什么能，中国特色社会主义为什么好，归根到底是马克思主义行，是中国化时代化的马克思主义行。习近平新时代中国特色社会主义思想是当代中国马克思主义、二十一世纪马克思主义，是中华文化和中国精神的时代精华，实现了马克思主义中国化时代化新的飞跃。中国过去五年极不寻常、极不平凡的成就和新时代十年的伟大变革，充分彰显了习近平新时代中国特色社会主义思想的真理力量和实践伟力。这一思想坚持把马克思主义基本原理同中国具体实际相结合、同中华优秀传统文化相结合，不断回答中国之问、世界之问、人民之问、时代之问，充分汲取中华优秀传统文化的精华养分，让马克思主义在中国牢牢扎根，推动科学社会主义在二十一世纪的中国焕发出新的蓬勃生机。

——**读懂中共二十大，就要读懂中国共产党自信自立的鲜明品格**。贯穿中国共产党百年奋斗的一个基本点，就是中国的问题必须从中国基本国情出发，由中国人自己来解答。只有植根本国、本民族历史文化沃土，马克思主义真理之树才能根深叶茂。中共二十大提出新时代新征程中国共产党的使命任务，明确以中国式现代化全面推进中华民族伟大复兴。中国式现代化，是中国共产党领导的社会主义现代化，既有各国现代化的共同特征，更有基于自己国情的中国特色。世界上既不存在定于一尊的现代化模式，也不存在放之四海而皆准的现代化标准。中国式现代化拓展了发展中国家走向现代化的途径，为人类对更好社会制度的探索提供了中国方案。

——**读懂中共二十大，就要读懂中国共产党胸怀天下的宽广情怀**。中国共产党是为中国人民谋幸福、为中华民族谋复兴的党，也是为人类谋进步、为世界谋大同的党。过去十年，中国坚定不移走和平发展道路，推动构建人类命运共同体，弘扬全人类共同价值，建设新型国际关系，坚定维护国际公平正义，倡导践行真正的多边主义，始终做世界和平的建设者、全球发展的贡献者、国际秩序的维护者，充分彰显了中国共产党胸怀天下的价值追求。当前，世界之变、时代之变、历史之变正以前所未有的方式展开，百年未有之大变局加速演进，世界进入新的动荡变革期，人类又一次站在历史的十字路口。这就更加需要我们共担维护和平责任，同走和平发展道路，朝着构建人类命运共同体的目标不断迈进，携手共创人类更加美好的未来。

女士们、先生们、朋友们！

新华社是中国国家通讯社，也是具有全球影响的世界性通讯社，联接中外、沟通世界是新华社的责任。我们将不断加强对外话语创新，更加"亲切""地道"地讲好中国故事、中国共产党故事、新时代故事，当好融通中外的"连心桥"。

新华社与中央党史和文献研究院都是各自领域的权威，长期以来保持着密切的合作关系。希望我们双方以今天的活动为契机，进一步加强交流互动，深化务实合作，发挥各自优势，为中国发展和人类进步作出更大贡献。

希望与会嘉宾深入研讨交流，分享真知灼见，为大家带来思考和启发。也希望今天的活动能够帮助大家进一步了解中共二十大，了解中国共产党和中国人民，进而共同推动新时代的中国与世界书写交融发展的新篇章。

最后，祝活动圆满成功，谢谢大家！

关键在党

办好中国的事,关键在党

黄一兵

中央党史和文献研究院副院长
中央党史和文献研究院国家高端智库理事会副理事长

中共二十大报告指出,全面建设社会主义现代化国家、全面推进中华民族伟大复兴,关键在党。这一重要论述,深刻揭示了党在新时代中国特色社会主义事业中的领导核心地位。

"关键在党"是过去我们为什么能够成功的重要经验,也是未来我们怎样才能继续成功的根本遵循。下面,围绕"关键在党"这个主题,我谈四点体会。

第一,关键在党是深刻的历史启示。了解中国,必须了解中国共产党。中国共产党一经诞生,就把为中国人民谋幸福、为中华民族谋复兴确立为自己的初心使命。一百多年来,中国共产党人紧紧围绕实现中华民族伟大复兴的历史主题,把国家、民族的命运扛在肩膀上,将小我消融于"大我",成为无怨的奉献者、无悔的牺牲者、无私的奋斗者和无畏的创造者。真理的追求与使命的担当交相辉映,让复兴之路群星璀璨,照亮了曾经是沉沉黑夜的中华民族的天空。毛泽东曾经充满信心地指出:中国人民将会看见,中国的命运一经操在人民自己手里,中国就将如太阳升起在东方那样,以自己辉煌的光焰普照大地,迅速地荡涤反动政府留下的污泥浊水,治好战争的创伤,建设起一个崭新的、强盛的、名副其实的人民共和国。

一百多年来,党的顽强奋斗从根本上改变了中国人民的前途命运,中国人民彻底摆脱了被欺负、被压迫、被奴役的命运,成为国家、社会和自己命运的主人，人民民主不断发展，十四亿多人口实现全面小康，人民群众对美好生活的向往不断变为现实。党的顽强奋斗开辟了实现中华民族伟大复兴的正确道路，中国从四分五裂、一盘散沙到高度统一、民族团结，从积贫积弱、一穷二白到全面小康、繁荣富强，从被动挨打、饱受欺凌到独立自主、坚定自信，仅用几十年时间就走完发达国家几百年走过的工业化历程，创造了经济快速发展和社会长期稳定两大奇迹。党的顽强奋斗展示了马克思主义的强大生命力，党坚持把马克思主义写在自己的旗帜上，不断推进马克思主义中国化时代化，用博大胸怀吸收人类创造的一切优秀文明成果，用中国化时代化的马克思主义引领中国的社会革命不断开拓进取。党的顽强奋斗深刻影响了世界历史进程，党领导人民成功走出了中国式现代化，创造了人类文明新形态，成为推动人类发展进步的重要力量。党的顽强奋斗锻造了走在时代前列的中国共产党，党坚持性质宗旨，坚定理想信念，坚守初心使命，形成了以伟大建党精神为源头的精神谱系，经过不懈努力，找到了自我革命这一跳出"治乱兴衰"历史周期率的答案，确保党永远不变质、不变色、不变味。

第二，关键在党是郑重的人民选择。 中国共产党是人民的党。为了人民的利益，从1921年到1949年，党领导的革命队伍中，有名可查的烈士就达370多万人。和平建设时期，在抗震救灾、抗洪抢险、应对突发事件等急难险重任务中，哪里有困难和危险，哪里就有共产党员。脱贫攻坚战中，1800多名党员、干部将生命定格在脱贫攻坚征程上。新冠肺炎疫情发生以来，近400名党员、干部为抗击疫情献出了宝贵生命。中国共产党代表中国最广大人民根本利益，没有任何自己特殊的利益，从来不代表任何利益集团、任何权势团体、任何特权阶层的利益，始终全心全意为人民服务，始终把人民放在第一位，不断把为人民造福的事业推向前进。

在党的领导下，今天的中国人民更加自信、自立、自强，极大增强了志气、骨气、底气，焕发出前所未有的历史主动精神、历史创造精神。今天的中国，人均GDP超过1万美元，形成了世界上规模最大的中等收入群体，建成了世界上规模最大的社会保障体系；今天的中国，城市繁华时尚，乡村和谐美丽，市场充满活力，社会安定有序。中国共产党顽强奋斗的根本目的，就是要把发展和进步写在物阜民丰的中华大地上，写在万家灯火的幸福日子里，写在共同富裕的美好追求中。

第三，关键在党是崇高的使命召唤。在近代中国社会出现的所有政党中，中国共产党是最早提出实现中华民族复兴的政党，是最早阐发中华民族复兴历史使命和任务的政党，而且是一以贯之为之接续奋斗。

党领导人民创造的新民主主义革命伟大成就，为实现中华民族伟大复兴创造了根本社会条件；党领导人民创造的社会主义革命和建设伟大成就，为实现中华民族伟大复兴奠定了根本政治前提和制度基础；党领导人民创造的改革开放和社会主义现代化建设伟大成就，为实现中华民族伟大复兴提供了充满新的活力的体制保证和快速发展的物质条件。

进入新时代，我们经历了对党和人民事业具有重大现实意义和深远历史意义的三件大事：一是迎来中国共产党成立一百周年，二是中国特色社会主义进入新时代，三是完成脱贫攻坚、全面建成小康社会的历史任务，实现第一个百年奋斗目标。这是中国共产党和中国人民团结奋斗赢得的历史性胜利，是彪炳中华民族发展史册的历史性胜利，也是对世界具有深远影响的历史性胜利。新时代十年，我们全面贯彻党的基本理论、基本路线、基本方略，采取一系列战略性举措，推进一系列变革性实践，实现一系列突破性进展，取得一系列标志性成果，经受住了来自政治、经济、意识形态、自然界等方面的风险挑战考验，党和国家事业取得历史性成就、发生历史性变革，推动我国迈上全面建设社会主义现代化国家新征程。中华民族迎来了从站起来、富起来到强起来的伟大飞跃，实现中华民族伟大复兴进入了不可逆转的历史进程。今天，我们比历史上任何时期都更接近、更有信心和能力实现中华民族伟大复兴的宏伟目标。

第四，关键在党是独有的清醒坚定。中国共产党在内外忧患中诞生，在磨难挫折中成长，在战胜风险挑战中壮大，始终有着强烈的忧患意识、风险意识。面对新形势新任务，习近平总书记告诫全党同志务必不忘初心、牢记使命，务必谦虚谨慎、艰苦奋斗，务必敢于斗争、善于斗争，坚定历史自信，增强历史主动。这不禁让人想起在中国革命即将取得全国性胜利的前夕，毛泽东对全党的谆谆教诲，他指出：夺取全国胜利，这只是万里长征走完了第一步，如果这一步也值得骄傲，那是比较渺小的。革命以后的路程更长，工作更伟大，更艰苦。这一点现在就必须向党内讲明白。

今天我们也可以说，相对于中华民族千秋伟业，一切过往皆是序章，未来依然充满各种风险挑战甚至惊涛骇浪。习近平总书记深刻指出：我们党作为世界上最大的马克思主义执政党，要始终赢得人民拥护、巩固长期执政地位，必须时刻保持解决大党独有难题的清醒和坚定。全党必须牢记全面从严治党永远在路上，党的自我革命永远在路上，决不能有松劲歇脚、疲劳厌战的情绪，必须持之以恒推进全面从严治党，深入推进新时代党的建设新的伟大工程，以党的自我革命继续引领社会革命。唯有矢志不渝、笃行不息，方能不负时代、不负人民。

中国人民深刻认识到，新时代十年的伟大变革，根本在于有习近平总书记作为党中央的核心、全党的核心掌舵领航，在于有习近平新时代中国特色社会主义思想科学指引。中国人民坚信，新征程上，深刻领悟"两个确立"的决定性意义，牢记"国之大者"，增强"四个意识"、坚定"四个自信"、做到"两个维护"，切实把党的领导落实到党和国家事业各领域各方面各环节，就一定能够开创党和国家事业发展的新局面。一个生机勃勃的中国共产党用伟大奋斗创造了百年伟业，也一定能用新的伟大奋斗创造新的伟业。

全面建设社会主义现代化国家关键在中国共产党
——理解中共二十大精神的一个重要视角

张贺福

中央党史和文献研究院第一研究部一级巡视员

习近平总书记在中国共产党第二十次全国代表大会上的报告中强调："全面建设社会主义现代化国家、全面推进中华民族伟大复兴，关键在党。"这句话内涵很深刻，是理解中共二十大精神一个十分重要的论断。我认为，至少可以从下述三个方面去把握。

第一，新时代十年创造的伟大成就、实现的伟大变革，关键在于中国共产党的领导。在百年奋斗历程中，中国共产党锻炼得越来越坚强有力，具有强大的政治领导能力、思想引领能力、号召组织能力。在新时代的十年来，中国共产党经受住了来自政治、经济、意识形态、自然界等各个方面风险挑战的考验，如期打赢了人类历史上规模最大的脱贫攻坚战，实现了小康这个中华民族的千年梦想，推动中国特色社会主义事业取得历史性成就、发生历史性变革，推动中国迈上全面建设社会主义现代化国家的新征程。所有这些成就的取得，最根本的在于中国共产党总揽全局、协调各方的坚强有力领导，在于有习近平这位党的总书记作为党中央的核心、全党的核心的掌舵领航，在于有习近平新时代中国特色社会主义思想的科学指引。中共二十大最重要的成果就是选举产生了以习近平同志为核心的新一届中央领导集体。有习近平总书记继续掌舵引航，中国这艘巨轮就会沿着正确方向，坚定不移、乘风破浪，实现大会确立的发展战略和目标。

第二，全面建设社会主义现代化国家、全面建成社会主义现代化强国，

关键在于中国共产党的领导。二十大报告指出，"从现在起，中国共产党的中心任务就是团结带领全国各族人民全面建成社会主义现代化强国、实现第二个百年奋斗目标，以中国式现代化全面推进中华民族伟大复兴。"强调："中国式现代化，是中国共产党领导的社会主义现代化。"报告在阐述中国式现代化的本质要求时，第一条就是强调"坚持中国共产党领导"。这些重要论断深刻阐述了中国式现代化最本质的特征、最大的优势。由于中国共产党始终代表最广大人民的根本利益，与人民休戚与共、生死相依，没有任何自己特殊的利益，从来不代表任何利益集团、任何权势团体、任何特权阶层的利益，因此能够在实践中不断显示出强大的先进性和纯洁性，能够吸引、凝聚最广大的中国人民在奋斗道路上不断取得一个又一个巨大成就，成功走出中国式现代化道路，创造了人类文明新形态。全面建设社会主义现代化国家、全面建成社会主义现代化强国面临的环境更复杂、要求更高，必须也只能坚持中国共产党的领导。

第三，全面建设社会主义现代化国家、全面建成社会主义现代化强国，必须建设坚强有力的党，关键在党要管党、全面从严治党。围绕全面从严治党、深入推进新时代党的建设新的伟大工程，二十大报告以解决大党独有难题的清醒和坚定，从七个方面作出周密安排。一是坚持和加强党中央集中统一领导，保证党的决策部署落实好，确保党的团结统一。二是持续不断地用习近平新时代中国特色社会主义思想这一党的最新理论创新成果，提高思想境界和认识水平、提高决策部署的能力、提高解决问题的能力，把党的最新理论创新成果转化为坚定理想、锤炼党性、指导实践、推动工作的强大力量。三是完善推进党的自我革命的制度规范体系，坚持和贯彻制度治党、依规治党，提高党的建设科学化水平。四是建设堪当民族复兴重任的高素质干部队伍，确保党的事业后继有人、不断向前推进。五是增强党组织的政治功能和组织功能，把中国共产党的优势充分发挥出来、力量迸发出来。六是坚持以严的基调端正党内风气、严格执行党的纪律，确保全体党员特别是领导干部都能够严于律己、严负其责。七是坚决打赢反腐败斗争攻坚战和持久战，清除危害党的最大毒瘤，按照党的性质、宗旨和实现奋斗目标的要求实行最彻底的自我革命。这些工作安排和要求，是中国共产党从全面建设社会主义现代化国家、全面建成社会主义现代化强国的奋斗目标出发，针对党内存在的问题，总结历史、立足当下、面向未来提出来的，对于中国共产党在领导推动现代化事业中始终保持自身的先进性、纯洁性和强大的执政能力至关重要。

跟着中国共产党走,是人民的选择、历史的必然

张旭东

新华社国内部副主任

尊敬的黄院长,

尊敬的各位嘉宾:

大家好!

很高兴有机会和大家分享我的观点。作为新华社研究院一名特约研究员,同时作为一名记者,我参加了这次中国共产党二十大的报道。参加大会的2300多名代表和特邀代表,既肩负9600多万名党员的信任重托,也承载14亿多人民的殷切期待——中国老百姓都知道,办好中国的事情,关键在党,跟着共产党走,就没有干不成的事。

——**跟着中国共产党走,亿万人民走上富裕之路**。江山就是人民,人民就是江山。习近平总书记在二十大报告中指出:"中国共产党领导人民打江山、守江山,守的是人民的心。"习近平总书记的话,揭示了中国共产党赢得民心、老百姓始终跟党走的奥秘。

二十大代表中,有一位来自农村的村支部书记,他叫裴春亮,今年52岁,他所在的河南辉县市裴寨村,地处太行山丘陵地带,曾是"省级贫困村"。中共十八大以来,裴春亮和村委把党小组建在农、工、商产业上,村民人均年收入翻了几番。裴春亮是千千万万带领老百姓致富的基层共产党员的一个缩影。

成立于1921年的中国共产党,初心和使命就是为中国人民谋幸福、为中华民族谋复兴。曾经被称为"东亚病夫"的中国老百姓,如今享受全世

界最大的民生保障网；人均预期寿命从新中国刚成立时的35岁增长到如今的78岁。在新时代十年的伟大变革中，为打赢脱贫攻坚战，全国累计选派25.5万个驻村工作队、300多万名第一书记和驻村干部，有1800多名同志为此献出了生命。经过8年艰苦卓绝的奋斗，我们夺取了这场人类历史上规模最大的脱贫攻坚战的胜利，近1亿农村贫困人口实现脱贫，在中华大地上全面建成了小康社会。

中国共产党就是人民的党。1945年，在中共七大上，"具有全心全意为中国人民服务的精神"这句话写进了党章。从"为人民服务"到"以人民为中心"，中国共产党始终以人民为标尺，持之以恒答好人民考卷。如今，站在发展的更高历史起点上，中国共产党已把促进全体人民共同富裕摆在了更加重要的位置，亿万中国人民正以中共二十大报告为行动指南，阔步走在全面建设社会主义现代化国家的新征程上。

——**跟着中国共产党走，古老中国走上复兴之路**。二十大召开前的一个月，我有机会来到上海的中共一大会址采访。好似时空穿越，令人感慨万千。百年前的中国，风雨飘摇，诸路皆走不通。1929年上海的《生活周刊》刊登一篇《十问未来之中国》的文章疾呼：吾国何时可稻产自丰、谷产自足，不忧饥馑？吾国何时可自产水笔、灯罩、自行表、人工车等物什，供国人生存之需？……此泣血呐喊，饱含国人渴盼："此十问俱实现，则中国富强矣"。

斗转星移，换了人间。谷物总产量世界第一、制造业规模世界第一、货物贸易总额世界第一……在中国共产党领导下，今天的中国焕发出蓬勃生机，已经创造并正在创造着一个又一个"第一"，已经创造并继续创造着一个又一个彪炳史册的人间奇迹。

我也参加过中共十八大、十九大的报道，真切感知到新时代中国铿锵的前进步伐。新时代十年的伟大变革，为实现中华民族伟大复兴提供了更为完善的制度保证、更为坚实的物质基础、更为主动的精神力量。今天的中国，实现中华民族伟大复兴进入了不可逆转的历史进程。

——**跟着中国共产党走，中华民族走上胜利之路**。中国共产党从一个只有50多名党员的组织，发展成为世界上最大的马克思主义执政党，团结带领亿万人民夺取了一个又一个伟大胜利。在我们现在所处的中国共产党历史展览馆中，有一个抗疫专题展区，悬挂着一面面写着"党员突击队"的旗帜，诠释着打赢武汉保卫战的密码。两年多前，在以习近平同志为核心的中共中央坚强领导下，举国动员打响这场疫情防控阻击战，总计有346支国家医疗队、4万多名医务人员奔赴湖北武汉，其中党员占了大多数。当时我也在武汉进行报道，采访本上记着这样一个数据，2020年2月9日是"逆行者"到达最多的一天，从12个省市飞来41架飞机，载有5787名支援者。身在武汉，我总是被这样一个个举全党举全国之力、气壮山河的举动所震撼、所感动。中国的老百姓始终相信：有党在，人民就有主心骨，就一定能战胜一切艰难险阻；跟着共产党走，中华民族定能继续创造令人刮目相看的伟大奇迹。

每次党代会，对中国发展都是一个里程碑。中共一大召开，中国人民形容这是"开天辟地"的大事。一百年后、如今召开的中共二十大，擘画了迈向全面建设社会主义现代化国家新征程、向第二个百年奋斗目标进军的宏伟蓝图，是中国踏上新征程的一件大事。

1940年，有一首创作于我的家乡山东沂蒙山革命老区的歌曲，传唱至今成为经典，歌词是这样写的："你是灯塔，照耀着黎明前的海洋；你是舵手，掌握着航行的方向。伟大的中国共产党，你就是核心，你就是方向。"这首歌曲的名字就叫《跟着共产党走》，歌曲唱出了人民的心声，也深刻昭示：跟着中国共产党走，是人民的选择、是历史的必然。

我的发言就到这里，谢谢大家！

解读中共二十大：中国共产党的关键作用

苏傲古

西班牙埃萨达商学院教授、"与中国对话项目"负责人

在北京中南海，正门位置有一块影壁，上面刻着"为人民服务"五个大字。这一理念是理解中国共产党的宗旨和当代中国治理体系的重要基础。今年，习近平主席在《习近平谈治国理政》第四卷里引用了一句十分重要的古语："为治之本，务在于安民；安民之本，在于足用。"① 换句话说，履行职责，造福人民。下面，我着重谈五点认识。

第一，体现效率，履行职责，造福人民。中国共产党不断推进为人民造福的事业，成绩斐然。2021年，中国宣布完成了消除绝对贫困的艰巨任务，在过去10年近1亿农村贫困人口全部脱贫。众所周知，中国在过去40年里使超过8.5亿人摆脱贫困。这个数字在人类历史上也是空前的，得到了联合国等国际组织的认可。

第二，以人民为中心的发展思想。到上个十年末，中国一些城市和农村地区的人均预期寿命与发达国家的差距明显缩小。2019年，北京市人均预期寿命已经达到82岁，而华盛顿降至77岁。这一统计数据已经足够惊人，但后续发展更出人意料。2022年9月的数据显示，中国人均预期寿命超过美国，这是中国特色国家治理体系的结晶，这一成就不仅应该令西方

---

① 该引语出自习近平主席在中华人民共和国恢复联合国合法席位五十周年纪念会上的讲话。见《习近平谈治国理政》（第四卷），北京：外文出版社2022年版，第475—476页。——编者注

瞩目，也应该令世界瞩目。

第三，系统全面的方法论。在过去的70年里，中国从一个农业国发展至今，拥有世界上规模最大的教育体系和社会保障体系，覆盖范围最广的高速铁路网和不同领域的尖端技术，这有赖于创新的发展理念、前瞻性思考和切实可行的长远规划。最近召开的中共二十大指出，中国在各领域取得辉煌成就，成为140多个国家和地区的主要贸易伙伴，货物贸易总额居世界第一。中国经济总量占世界经济的比重达18.5%，在过去10年中提高7.2个百分点。

第四，保持自身特色。鉴于过去几十年中国取得的发展成就，一些国际分析人士可能会认为，中国是在倡导本国发展模式，或试图说服其他国家效仿。但习近平主席多次强调，各个国家都有各自的国情。一个国家不考虑本国国情而试图照搬外国模式是不明智的。中国依靠自己的历史、规模和文化，包括政治文化，一直坚持走中国特色社会主义道路。中国领导人再次强调，中国式现代化道路走得好，它不是西方现代化的翻版。当然，这对于世界各地的国际事务分析人士来说都是不争的事实。

第五，灵活性。正如习近平主席最近在中共二十大上所说的那样，"坚持道不变、志不改，既不走封闭僵化的老路，也不走改旗易帜的邪路"。他的这番话是对中国所走的成功道路的高度认可。在过去的几十年里，中国从世界舞台边缘稳步迈向舞台中央，体现了不断前进的毅力和对自身未来发展的信心。

中国式现代化与共同富裕

肖 恩

中央党史和文献研究院外国专家（英文）

女士们，先生们：

大家下午好！

中国过去几十年的发展，关键在于中国共产党的领导。中国共产党不仅带领中国消除了绝对贫困，在未来几十年里，还将在中国实现共同富裕的道路上继续发挥关键作用。习近平主席指出，共同富裕是中国式现代化的重要特征。中国共产党将共同富裕作为其以人为本发展理念的重要支撑，是其为人民服务总体目标的关键所在，也是中国发展的最终目标。

过去十年里，中国在促进共同富裕方面成绩斐然。我妻子的蛋糕店让我对这些成绩有了一定的了解。五年前她刚开店时，更高质量的消费基础刚刚形成。我妻子为产品选用了优质的原料，也就意味着要收取更高的价格。当时，她产品的消费群体主要是拥有一定可支配收入的年轻人和高收入的白领。所以起初，业务的增长低于预期。但近几年里，她的业务不断扩大，客户群也覆盖了社会的各个阶层。

业务增长的原因之一是人民生活水平的提高。人们有了更高的收入，就更能为自己的生活增加一些额外的甜头，除了蛋糕和甜点，还包括各种更高质量的产品和服务消费。人均可支配年收入的增长也体现了这一点。过去的十年里，人均可支配年收入从 16500 元增长到了 35100 元。

居民收入的增长和有利的营商环境为企业蓬勃发展创造了条件。科技创新和现代物流也发挥了重要作用，企业既能接触更多客户，又能降低成本。随着企业的不断发展，用工人数也在持续增加。一开始，我妻子只雇用了三四个人，现在已经扩充到20人。所有雇员都缴纳了社保，收入年年攀升。

但这只是故事的一小部分罢了。过去十年里，中国农村地区的变化更是让人印象深刻。精准扶贫让中国9899万农村贫困人口、832个贫困县和12.8万个贫困村全部摆脱贫困。中国共产党把脱贫攻坚作为首要任务，践行了自己全面建设小康社会路上"决不能落下一个贫困地区、一个贫困群众"的承诺。

通过增进民生福祉、促进区域协调发展、消除绝对贫困、实现全面小康，中国共产党为未来几十年中国向共同富裕迈进奠定了坚实基础。

中国共产党表示，今后将继续加大力度解决地区差距、城乡差距、收入分配差距等问题。这些措施也是把"蛋糕"做大、把"蛋糕"分好战略的一部分。归根到底，这就需要协调好公平和效率之间的关系。

对任何社会和制度而言，保持这种平衡都是一项长期的、有很大难度的挑战。作为执政党，中国共产党在确保中国能够平衡这两种因素方面发挥了至关重要的作用。我认为，中国共产党之所以能够有效履行这一职责，有以下几个原因：

首先，中国共产党在应对促进效率与公平面临的挑战方面积累了大量经验。这就意味着，中国共产党做好了万全准备，能够应对各种暗中隐藏的陷阱。比如说，中国共产党已明确表示，共同富裕不是平均主义。中国共产党将继续坚持以人民群众勤劳创新致富为重点，同时也将确保政府更好发挥其作用，保障好基本民生、为人民服务。

其次，将共同富裕作为长期奋斗的目标。习近平主席强调，共同富裕需要一个过程，等不得，也急不得。今后几十年，中国朝着共同富裕的目标坚定不移地循序迈进，就能在统筹公平和效率方面创造出一片广阔天地。

最后，中国共产党先在地方试点后在全国推广的做法同样至关重要。浙江已推进了共同富裕示范区建设。其余各地也在探索共同富裕的创新发展模式。我认为，这种地方实验为创新解决方案、完善政策规定、解决潜在问题等创造了机会。

　　总的来说,过去十年里取得的成就让中国能够在未来向着共同富裕的目标大步迈进。我妻子的生意前景也是一片光明,因为她都在筹备开第二家店了。

　　谢谢大家!

中国共产党在各个领域的关键作用

舍拉迪尔·巴克特古洛夫

吉尔吉斯斯坦国家战略研究所顾问

中国共产党向世界证明,共产主义在现代世界非常有效。中国共产党第二十次全国代表大会是今年中国最重大的事件。中国多年来取得的成就很大程度上归功于中国共产党。中国共产党的领导角色使中国人摆脱了"屈辱世纪"的枷锁,发展了自己的经济,成为世界公认的经济强国,并为普遍公平发展建立了模型。

因为中国共产党的执政成就,许多国家再次把注意力转向了中国创造的独特治理模式,这种模式利用市场经济的优势并依赖每个公民的支持。中国消除了绝对贫困,全面建成小康社会,正朝着建成社会主义现代化强国的第二个百年奋斗目标前进。

中国共产党一直遵循自己的初心。中华民族伟大复兴已成为不可逆转的历史进程。全面建成小康社会是中国共产党百年来成功实现的一个美好目标。而如今中国共产党正在带领中国人民努力实现第二个百年目标:到本世纪中叶把中国建设成为富强民主文明和谐美丽的社会主义现代化强国。

全面建成小康社会是中国共产党对人民的重要承诺。这项任务的完成不仅意味着将国家经济、科技力量提升到一个新的水平,提高全体人民的生活水平,而且意味着能够与国际社会分享中国智慧和中国方案。

中国共产党二十大提出,以中国式现代化全面推进中华民族伟大复兴。值得注意的是,中国式现代化意味着全体中国人生活水平的提高,在共同富裕的道路上没有人会被落下。

中共二十大报告指出,"我们坚定站在历史正确的一边、站在人类文明进步的一边,高举和平、发展、合作、共赢旗帜,在坚定维护世界和平与发展中谋求自身发展,又以自身发展更好维护世界和平与发展。"的确,一个世纪以来,中国共产党在中华民族发展史和人类进步史上写下了光辉篇章。一代代中国共产党人,为国家独立、强大和民众福祉而奋斗,并与其他国家分享其经验,包括消除贫困领域的经验。中国国家主席习近平多次在全球层面呼吁构建人类命运共同体,建设持久和平、普遍安全、共同繁荣、开放包容、清洁美丽的世界。

中国提出"一带一路"倡议,旨在通过协调一致的政策、互联互通的基础设施、自由贸易和投资金融合作以及人文交流来加强国家之间的联系。通过这一倡议,中国向世界提供公共产品,提倡以和平合作、开放包容、互学互鉴、互利共赢为核心的丝路精神。

二十大报告指出,"共建'一带一路'成为深受欢迎的国际公共产品和国际合作平台。中国成为一百四十多个国家和地区的主要贸易伙伴,货物贸易总额居世界第一,吸引外资和对外投资居世界前列,形成更大范围、更宽领域、更深层次对外开放格局。"以共商共建共享为原则推动"一带一路"倡议,展现出中国共产党的开放性。

如果我们分析中国共产党的百年历史,不难看出,中国共产党一向对外界的思想持开放态度。中国共产党不仅长期坚持不懈在争取民族解放的艰难斗争中发挥最大作用,而且在新中国成立后,特别是20世纪70年代末实行改革开放政策后,努力完善国家治理。

得益于中国共产党领导人向发达国家学习的意愿,中国找到了一条与国情相适应的发展道路,并在实行改革开放后的30年内发展成为世界第二大经济体,提高了民众的生活水平,为全球经济增长作出了贡献。改革开放以来,中国有8.5亿多人摆脱贫困,提前十年实现了联合国可持续发展议程中提出的2030年消除贫困的目标。

中国共产党二十大呼吁全体人民为全面建设社会主义现代化国家、全面推进中华民族伟大复兴而团结奋斗。相信在中国共产党的领导下，在中国共产党富有远见的政策指导下，拥有无限潜能的中国人民一定能实现这个目标。

中国式现代化

以中国式现代化全面推进中华民族伟大复兴

赵 承

新华通讯社副社长
新华社国家高端智库学术委员会执行副主任

刚刚闭幕的中共二十大描绘了全面建设社会主义现代化国家、全面推进中华民族伟大复兴的宏伟蓝图。在这次大会上,习近平总书记深刻阐述了中国式现代化的科学内涵、中国特色和本质要求,强调坚持以中国式现代化全面推进中华民族伟大复兴。

在这里,我愿同大家分享对这个议题的一些认识。

第一个问题:中国成功推进和拓展了中国式现代化。

现代化是人类进入工业文明以来的共同追求,也是近代以来中华民族孜孜以求的梦想。中国共产党成立一百多年来,团结带领中国人民所进行的一切奋斗,就是为了把中国建设成为现代化强国,实现中华民族伟大复兴。在新中国成立特别是改革开放以来的长期探索和实践基础上,经过中共十八大以来在理论和实践上的创新突破,我们成功推进和拓展了中国式现代化。

过去10年间,中国共产党领导中国人民打赢了人类历史上规模最大的脱贫攻坚战,让近1亿农村贫困人口实现脱贫,改变了无数普通中国人的命运。

最近,我们在采访中了解到一名生活在中国西南大凉山区的女孩吉好有果的故事。那里,平均海拔超过2500米,曾经家家户户都住在山梁上的土房里,被称为"中国贫困的角落"。10岁以前的吉好有果,从没见过山外的世界，住的是低矮、昏暗、破败的土坯房，晚上下雨的时候，雨都会漏出来。现在，已经14岁的吉好有果，全家住进了100平方米的新楼房，她也走出大山到城里上初中。在大凉山区，有100多万像吉好有果这样的贫困人口脱了贫，开启了充满希望的生活。

彻底解决了绝对贫困问题，是中国推进现代化道路上迈出的一大步。中国仅用几十年时间就走完发达国家几百年走过的工业化历程，创造了世所罕见的经济快速发展和社会长期稳定两大奇迹。2021年，中国经济总量超过114万亿元，占世界经济比重达18.5%，人均国内生产总值接近高收入国家门槛，建成世界上规模最大的教育体系、社会保障体系、医疗卫生体系。今天，中国有世界最大的高速铁路网、高速公路网，在载人航天、探月探火、量子信息、新能源技术等领域也取得了重大成就。

中共二十大报告对全面建成社会主义现代化强国明确了"分两步走"的战略安排，从2020年到2035年，基本实现社会主义现代化；从2035年到本世纪中叶，把中国建成富强民主文明和谐美丽的社会主义现代化强国。

第二问题：深刻把握中国式现代化的中国特色。

中国式现代化，是中国共产党领导的社会主义现代化，既有各国现代化的共同特征，更有基于自己国情的中国特色。中共二十大报告概括了中国式现代化的5个中国特色，即人口规模巨大的现代化；全体人民共同富裕的现代化；物质文明和精神文明相协调的现代化；人与自然和谐共生的现代化；走和平发展道路的现代化。

迄今为止，全世界实现现代化的国家和地区总人口不超过10亿人。中国14亿多人口整体迈入现代化社会，将使世界上迈入现代化的人口翻一番多，将彻底改写现代化的世界版图。中国式现代化的艰巨性和复杂性前所未有，发展途径和推进方式也必然具有自己的特点。

中国文化始终注重天人合一，强调人与自然是生命共同体。中国不走"先污染后治理"的现代化老路，像保护眼睛一样保护自然和生态环境，坚定不移走生产发展、生活富裕、生态良好的文明发展道路。

这里可以举一个例子：中国长江里的江豚已在地球上生存了2500万年，

它是长江中唯一的哺乳动物,被喻为"水中大熊猫",曾经几近绝迹。前几天,中国农业农村部公布了2022年长江全流域江豚科学考察的初步结果。科考队员在长江的上中下游多处可喜地发现了十几头的江豚大群体,尤其是母子豚的数量显著增多,甚至过去分布空白的流段也发现了江豚。现在,长江这条中国最大的河流正实施"十年禁渔",沿江20余万渔民转产上岸,让母亲河休养生息。

中国式现代化坚持把实现人民对美好生活的向往作为现代化建设的出发点和落脚点,着力维护和促进社会公平正义,不断促进物的全面丰富和人的全面发展,既创造更多物质财富和精神财富,也提供更多优质生态产品以满足人民日益增长的优美生态环境需要。

第三个问题:牢牢把握中国式现代化的本质要求。

中共二十大报告提出了中国式现代化的9条本质要求:坚持中国共产党领导,坚持中国特色社会主义,实现高质量发展,发展全过程人民民主,丰富人民精神世界,实现全体人民共同富裕,促进人与自然和谐共生,推动构建人类命运共同体,创造人类文明新形态。

准确把握这些本质要求,才能读懂中国如何以中国式现代化全面推进中华民族伟大复兴。

从本质特征看,中国式现代化是中国共产党领导的社会主义现代化。坚持中国共产党的领导,是中国式现代化最鲜明的特征和最突出的优势,是推进中国式现代化必须坚持的最高原则。坚持中国特色社会主义,是推进中国式现代化的最本质要求。

从科学内涵看,推进中国式现代化的奋斗目标就是建成富强民主文明和谐美丽的社会主义现代化强国,这就必须全面提升物质文明、政治文明、精神文明、社会文明、生态文明水平。其中,全面提升物质文明水平,必须坚持以实现高质量发展为方向。中共二十大报告把高质量发展明确作为全面建设社会主义现代化国家的首要任务,进一步凸显了发展质量的全局和长远意义。

从国际影响看,以和平方式实现国家发展和民族复兴,是中国式现代化的显著特征。中国式现代化拓展了发展中国家走向现代化的途径，开辟了一条合作共赢、共建共享的文明发展新道路，为解决人类问题贡献了中国智慧和中国方案。

这里我分享一位中共二十大代表的故事：来自中国福建省一所大学的菌草专家林占熺，今年已经79岁了，一辈子专注研究如何"以草代木"养菇致富、治理风沙甚至发电造纸。30多年来，他把自己研发的菌草种到了中国的沙漠里、戈壁滩、黄河边，随后推广至全球100多个国家和地区，从南太岛国到非洲、拉美，许多人通过种菌草、种菇，摆脱了贫困。这正是中国通过走中国式现代化道路，以自身发展更好惠及各国人民的缩影。

一个有着5000多年历史的古老文明阔步迈向现代化，堪称这个蓝色星球上精彩的奋斗故事、引人注目的文明史诗。在中国共产党领导下，中国人民充满自信地以中国式现代化全面推进中华民族伟大复兴，中国发展新答卷必将让世界对中国道路有全新的认识。

"中国式现代化"概念及翻译

张士义

中央党史和文献研究院第六研究部主任

"中国式现代化"是中共二十大报告中的核心概念之一。习近平总书记讲过多次,二十大报告又专门系统阐述了它的中国特色和本质要求。对此,大会代表讨论热烈,国内外舆论也高度关注。

这不难理解。因为我们已经全面建成小康社会、实现了第一个百年奋斗目标。接下来我们的任务是全面建设社会主义现代化国家,朝着第二个百年奋斗目标前进。也就是说,实现现代化已经成为我们的直接目标和现实任务。

应该说,现代化是全人类共同追求的目标之一。西方发达国家已经实现了现代化。包括中国在内的广大发展中国家,正在为实现现代化而奋斗。新中国成立以来,经过长期探索和实践,特别是进入新时代以来,我们党对建设社会主义现代化国家在认识上不断深入、战略上不断成熟、实践上不断丰富,成功推进和拓展了中国式现代化,创造了人类文明新形态。中国式现代化扎根中国大地,切合中国实际,具有巨大发展潜力。

中国之所以能够走出新的现代化道路,是因为我们有"独特的文化传统,独特的历史命运,独特的基本国情",这"注定了我们必然要走适合自己特点的发展道路"。

我们还可以从以下两个方面来理解:一是中国是个大国,大就要有大的样子,这就是要独立自主决定自己的未来,既不能跟风,也不能骑墙,而必须走自己的路,"要始终把国家和民族发展放在自己力量的基点上、把中国发展进步的命运牢牢掌握在自己手中"。二是在人类实现现代化的历史进程中，中国是一个后发国家，既可以学习借鉴发达国家现代化的有益经验，又能够避免它们走过的弯路、经历的曲折、留下的斑斑劣迹，从而在中国式现代化道路上发展得更快、更稳、更好，创造出经济快速发展和社会长期稳定的奇迹。可以说，中国式现代化的推进和拓展，既彰显了中国特色社会主义的巨大优越性，又打破了"现代化就是西方化"的神话，为其他发展中国家实现现代化提供了新的选择。

怎样看待报告中关于"中国式现代化"的论述？我想，关键是理解和把握它的性质和定位。

报告指出，中国式现代化是中国共产党领导的社会主义现代化。这句话清楚地说明了中国式现代化的性质——它不同于西方国家以资本为中心的资本主义现代化，而是以人民为中心的社会主义现代化。它秉承了中国文化传统，能够克服资本主义社会因资本逐利最大化所造成的贫富悬殊、物质主义、消费主义等弊端。它倡导实现"人的全面发展"，而不是资本主义制度下形成的"单向度的人"。

报告还阐述了中国式现代化的5大特征和9条本质要求。这些论述有助于我们理解中国式现代化的定位——它是相对于西方式现代化而言的，是一个独立、完整、高规格的大概念。基于以上认识，我们在对外翻译"中国式现代化"这个概念时，英文使用了"Chinese modernization"这个译法。这种译法言简意赅、语义直达，也适用于其他语言的翻译，便于在国际语境中传播。从二十大期间国际主要媒体的报道和评价看，这个英文译法得到普遍认可和使用，很快在国际社会传播开来，达到了预期的传播效果。

民族复兴和人民幸福：理解"中国式现代化"的两把钥匙

杨明伟

中央党史和文献研究院对外合作交流局局长

习近平总书记在谈到中国共产党人的"发展观"和"现代化观"时，明确指出："为人民谋幸福、为民族谋复兴，这既是我们党领导现代化建设的出发点和落脚点，也是新发展理念的'根'和'魂'。只有坚持以人民为中心的发展思想，坚持发展为了人民、发展依靠人民、发展成果由人民共享，才会有正确的发展观、现代化观。"他同时强调，我们就是坚持这样的发展观和现代化观，在长期探索实践基础上，成功推进和拓展中国式现代化的。

这就清楚地表明了中国式现代化与人民幸福、民族复兴的紧密联系。

一、中国式现代化是与中华民族伟大复兴紧紧连在一起的

中国式现代化与中华民族伟大复兴有着不可分割的内在联系，它是伴随着中华民族伟大复兴的历史进程一步步走来并全面深化发展的。中国共产党自建立以来，团结带领中国人民所进行的一切奋斗，就是为了把中国建设成为现代化强国，实现中华民族伟大复兴。新时代中国共产党人的使命任务，也是以中国式现代化全面推进中华民族伟大复兴。

中国共产党对中国式现代化的认识是随着实现民族复兴的探索逐步深化的。自中国共产党全国执政以来，始终坚定地沿着建设社会主义现代化国家、实现中华民族伟大复兴的清晰目标前进。为此，中国共产党领导国

家一开始就按照一个一个的五年计划（规划）和一段一段的远景目标设想，逐步推动经济社会向前发展、逐步朝着现代化国家的目标迈进。尽管我们最初对"现代化"内涵的理解还不够全面，但走向"现代化"的目标是确定的，认识也是不断发展的。早在1964年，在研究第三个五年计划过程中，中国共产党就提出了分两步走的战略安排，即从第三个五年计划开始，第一步用15年时间建立一个独立的比较完整的工业体系和国民经济体系，第二步，再用15年时间，在20世纪末实现工业、农业、国防和科学技术"四个现代化"的目标。进入改革开放新时期，我们党进一步提出建设富强、民主、文明的社会主义现代化国家的宏伟目标。中国特色社会主义进入新时代，我们党在更高的起点上从十九大开始提出了新的"两步走"战略，确定从2020年到2035年，在全面建成小康社会的基础上，再奋斗15年，基本实现社会主义现代化；从2035年到本世纪中叶，在基本实现现代化的基础上，再奋斗15年，把我国建成为富强民主文明和谐美丽的社会主义现代化强国。中共二十大重申了全面建成社会主义现代化强国的"两步走"战略安排。

从中国式现代化与中华民族伟大复兴的逻辑关系中，可以清晰地看出：中国共产党对建设社会主义现代化国家在认识上不断深入、在战略上不断成熟、在实践上不断丰富；党和人民建设社会主义现代化国家的意志和决心始终没有动摇。历史已经证明并还将证明，中国式现代化的发展逻辑和历史进程已经不可逆转，以中国式现代化推动中华民族伟大复兴这一历史进程也不可逆转。

二、中国式现代化的一个重要目标是共同富裕

共同富裕，是人民幸福的一个重要标志。而实现全体人民共同富裕，既是我们党对自己一以贯之的要求，也是中国式现代化的本质要求。中国共产党人对共同富裕的追求由来已久。

走向共同富裕的问题，是马克思主义理论所要解决的一个基本问题，是马克思、恩格斯对社会主义和共产主义社会状况的一个基本设想。中国

共产党一经成立，就自觉扛起了解决这个基本问题、实现这个基本设想的历史重任。新中国成立后，毛泽东主席曾提出过：在中国共产党领导下，中国"是可以一年一年走向更富更强的，一年一年可以看到更富、更强些。而这个富，是共同的富，这个强，是共同的强，大家都有份"。自20世纪80年代初期起，在改革开放的背景下，邓小平同志不断提醒人们："我们坚持走社会主义道路，根本目标是实现共同富裕。"中国特色社会主义进入新时代后，以习近平同志为核心的党中央把"扎实推进共同富裕"的问题提到了突出位置，着重强调"实现共同富裕，是中国特色社会主义的本质要求，是中国共产党的重要使命"，"必须更加注重共同富裕问题"，"朝着实现全体人民共同富裕的目标稳步迈进"。

自2020年中国脱贫攻坚战取得全面胜利，全面进入小康社会后，中国共产党在团结带领人民创造美好生活、实现共同富裕的道路上迈出了坚实的一大步。中国在解决困扰中华民族几千年的绝对贫困问题上取得了伟大历史性成就，创造了人类减贫史上的奇迹。为全面建设社会主义现代化国家打下了坚实的基础，也为实现第二个百年奋斗目标准备了条件。

可以肯定地说，能举全党全国之力让人民彻底摆脱贫困，只有在中国共产党的坚强领导下才能够真正实现；而带领人民由摆脱贫困逐步走向共同富裕，也只有中国共产党人能够承担这样的历史重任，最终解决这个重大课题。

以公平公正为核心：中国式现代化的前进方向

马丁·雅克

英国知名学者、中国问题专家

中国共产党第二十次全国代表大会上提到最有趣的问题之一就是中国式现代化。

现代化这一主题以及现代化遇到的问题，都不禁令人联想到19世纪初的中国。当时的中国未能与英国和其他欧洲国家同步走上工业化道路，甚至短时间之后也未能实现工业化。

事实上，直到150年后，从1949年新中国成立开始，中国才真正开启现代化战略。这在很大程度上展现了中国共产党的不懈努力。1949年后，特别是1978年后，邓小平及之后的领导人坚持现代化战略，推动经济发展，带领中国走向世界。

这段时期中国的现代化进程不可避免地受到西方影响，中国也不得不在一定程度上学习甚至模仿西方模式，因为这在当时来看是最恰当的选择。但这并不意味着直接照搬西方模式，因为中国必须根据自身国情调整现代化发展模式。所以中国一直在走有中国特色的发展道路，即使在这个时期也是如此。

尽管如此，我认为从整体上来说，迄今为止，现代化很大程度上建立在西方模式基础上。

现在，中共二十大提出一个非常有趣的问题，那就是尽管中国还没有达到美国的水平，但在某些领域，中国已经超越了美国。在技术方面，中国的创新能力很强。在经济方面，中国目前是世界第二大经济体，以某些计量标准衡量，中国已经是世界最大经济体。

因此，现在我们要重新思考现代化的本质。

什么是最适合中国的现代化？什么是最适合社会主义国家的现代化？

我认为这个问题非常关键，因为它为中国未来发展带来了无数种新的可能。但我现在不想长篇大论，我只举一个例子，那就是共同富裕。我认为，共同富裕确实可以解决中国在发展过程中遇到的许多问题，尤其是在经济高速增长导致社会不平等加剧时期。中国的基尼系数可能与美国相当。这对于一个社会主义国家来说，从长远来看，显然是需要调整的。中国需要大幅降低基尼系数，建立一个包容性社会，一个以公平公正为核心的先进社会。

所以我认为，中国式现代化的核心理念是建设更公平的社会。

这种理念对中国国际地位的影响也很值得探讨。因为在美国式全球化的整个时期，以美国为首全世界范围内都出现了不平等现象。而中国在某种程度上也被卷入其中，因为当时世界的现代化模式就是这样。

现在，在中国选择了一种完全不同的、以公正和平等为核心的现代化之后，会发生什么？

我认为，如果中国能像成功消除极端贫困一样成功实现这种现代化，那么中国这种以发展、公平、平等为核心的理念将对世界产生巨大影响。

中国式现代化为世界带来启发

福佩吉

中央党史和文献研究院外国专家（法文）

中国式现代化是中共二十大报告中一个突出的重要术语。中国式现代化既包含了各国现代化的共同元素，又具有符合中国国情的独特特征。

今天，我想与大家分享我对中国式现代化道路的理解。我认为，中国式现代化道路可以启发其他国家，为世界提供新的选择和机遇。

一、中国实践表明现代化可以有不同路径

2001 年中国加入世界贸易组织时，一些人，尤其一些西方人士，认为中国要走且只能走西方的现代化道路。这是对中国的一种误解。

中国从不想复制西方的现代化模式，也不想把自己的模式强加给其他国家。中国想要走自己的道路实现现代化，这是一种以人民为中心、高度重视保护环境、促进和平发展的社会主义现代化。此外，中国愿意与世界分享其经验和益处。

二、西方国家的现代化道路存在重大缺陷

西方现代化主要为生活在西方发达国家的少数世界人口提供物质财富，其基础是对绝大多数人的剥削、帝国主义、殖民主义和霸权主义。它造成了更多的社会不平等、剥削、战争、领土扩张、压迫其他人口、

浪费自然资源、污染、不平衡和不可持续的发展，等等。这不是中国想要走的道路。

三、中国式现代化不同于西方模式，适合中国国情

中国式现代化是适合中国国情、走中国特色社会主义道路、依靠人民、造福人民的现代化。它推动的发展不是仅为1%或10%的人带来共同富裕，甚至也不是仅为中国大多数人，而是为全体人民带来共同富裕。

中国式现代化也在扭转以牺牲环境为代价的发展趋势，推进一种遵循人与自然和谐共生的平衡、高质量和可持续性的发展。在发展过程中，生产、人民福祉和环境保护被视为不可分割的一个整体。

而且，中国式现代化不是走帝国主义、殖民主义、霸权主义的道路，而是走和平发展的道路。事实上，中国的发展建立在合作、平等、相互尊重、互利共赢的基础上。"一带一路"倡议就是一个具体的例子，这个倡议是中国发起的，它指的是共同发展，与各国共享发展成果。

最后，中国式现代化用中国智慧和中国方式提出解决人类面临的共同问题的方案。它运用马克思主义的观点和方法，以及一些进步的中国传统观念，分析世界，解决当今中国和其他国家面临的问题，例如，中国传统观念"天下一家"和马克思主义"每个人的自由发展是一切人的自由发展的条件"的观点。

四、中国式现代化对世界的影响越来越大

中国式现代化已经并将继续对世界产生越来越大的影响，不仅因为它有助于其他国家的发展，特别是那些在西方现代化进程中被掠夺和落下的发展中国家的发展，还因为它表明其他国家有可能走一条不同于西方的现代化道路，这条新道路可以为其他国家提供实现本国现代化的双赢途径；他们可以从中国的现代化经验中，根据他们自己的情况和需要，选择适合他们的要素，在保持独立自主的同时继续发展。

因此，中国在追求自身现代化的同时，也提供了一条新的现代化道路，可以为其他国家提供启示，为促进人类进步、世界和平与发展、建设生态文明和构建人类命运共同体作出更大贡献。

中国式现代化和全球合作

哈利德·阿克拉姆

巴基斯坦全球战略研究中心执行主任

人类命运共同体巴基斯坦研究中心主任

我叫哈利德·阿克拉姆，是巴基斯坦全球战略研究中心执行主任、人类命运共同体巴基斯坦研究中心主任。首先，衷心感谢本次论坛的主办方能够举办这样一场盛会，为大家齐聚一堂、共同解读中国共产党第二十次全国代表大会的成果提供很好的平台。感谢你们的邀请。接下来，我想与大家分享我对中国式现代化和未来合作可能性的看法。

世界各国在现代化进程中都面临挑战，但中国在习近平主席富有卓见的领导下，一直朝着现代化的目标奋勇向前。过去十年，中国的现代化发展极为迅速。现代化可以被定义为一个传统或欠发达社会向现代化和工业化社会的转变。中国经济的快速发展反映了这种转变。

在中国走向现代化的第一阶段，领导层的目标是结束旧有体制，建立人民共和国。在第二阶段，领导层探索新的治理机制，并着重通过工业化实现经济复苏。在第三阶段，自大规模推行改革开放以来，领导层的主要目标一直是创造务实的发展理念，并将国家议程考虑在内。在过去的几年里，领导层的目标是使中国成为一个现代化国家，实现中国梦。

我认为，改革开放和强有力的规划，使中国从高度集中的计划经济转变为全面的、多产业的市场经济，从过去人们眼中高度封闭的国家，变成了世界上最具活力和最开放的经济体之一。中国也历史性地从一个生产力落后的国家，跃居为世界第二大经济体，人民生活水平由低水平提高到小康水平。这些成就为快速发展创造了良好的制度条件和后期物质基础，推动国家走向现代化。

各位朋友，当今世界正在发生深刻变化，经济建设和现代化建设不仅促进了世界经济增长，也深化了广泛的全球合作。然而，现代化和全球化也带来了诸多挑战，特别是对一些发展中国家来说，这些挑战仍有待解决。在这方面，中国的发展治理体系和现代化模式对其他国家有借鉴意义，可以用来应对各自在现代化道路上面临的挑战。中国特色社会主义明确了领导层治国理政的方法。中国特色社会主义的本质是发展社会生产力。

我认为，中国的软实力在进一步推动现代化建设中也发挥了作用。中国大力提升软实力，使其能够屹立于世界舞台。的确，伟大的愿景是简单而纯粹的，但得通过行动才能变成现实。无论一项计划有多么实际、多么合理，如实施不当，就不会成功。因此，中国式现代化代表着国家经济、政治和社会的深刻渐进变化。这些变化并不是对现有价值和规范的否定，相反，它意味着现有社会在进行改革。

最后，我还想评价一下成功召开的中国共产党第二十次全国代表大会。作为世界上最具活力和最受欢迎的领导人，习近平主席将继续领导中国。我相信，在他的领导和强有力政策下，中国将增强其全球影响力，致力于未来五年的发展规划，将会激发热情并取得胜利。

非常感谢！

中华优秀传统文化

关于中华优秀传统文化

王均伟

中央党史和文献研究院学术和编审委员会主任（副部长级）
中央党史和文献研究院国家高端智库理事会执行副理事长

各位尊敬的嘉宾，

女士们，先生们：

大家下午好！

习近平总书记在中共二十大报告中指出："中国共产党人深刻认识到，只有把马克思主义基本原理同中国具体实际相结合、同中华优秀传统文化相结合，坚持运用辩证唯物主义和历史唯物主义，才能正确回答时代和实践提出的重大问题，才能始终保持马克思主义的蓬勃生机和旺盛活力。"

中华优秀传统文化历史悠久，内涵丰富，要在有限的时间内讲清楚是很困难的，我今天着重讲三点认识，同大家交流。

一、中华优秀传统文化是中华民族生生不息的强大精神支撑

中国有 5000 多年的文明史，培育和发展了独具特色、博大精深的中华文化，这些优秀的传统文化深入中国人的骨髓里，流淌在中国人的血液里，已经成为中华民族的遗传基因。为什么说这些文化生生不息？因为一直到今天，这些文化依然被中国人传承、敬仰、运用。孔子是 2500 多年前的人物，他写的书、讲的话，今天的中国人不仅在看、在学，而且在用来规范

自己的行为。我很高兴今天的论坛有这么多全世界各国的朋友来参加，这就是孔子说的"有朋自远方来，不亦乐乎"。中国不愿意被霸权主义欺凌，中国也从不欺负小国弱国，这也是孔子说过的"己所不欲，勿施于人"的体现。中华文化具有强大的韧性和魅力。历史上，北方游牧民族多次入主中原，最后都被中华文化折服，接受并丰富了中华文化，自身也成为中华民族大家庭的组成部分。所以说，中国的文化传统里，没有国强必霸的基因，中国永远不会成为霸权主义的国家。中华优秀传统文化中蕴含的天下为公、民为邦本、为政以德、革故鼎新、任人唯贤、天人合一、自强不息、厚德载物、讲信修睦、亲仁善邻，等等，都是中国人民在长期生产生活中积累的宇宙观、天下观、社会观、道德观的重要体现，是中华民族的宝贵精神财富和精神支撑。

二、中国共产党是中华优秀传统文化的传承者和弘扬者

80多年前，中国共产党力量还很弱小的时候，毛泽东就提出："从孔夫子到孙中山，我们应当给以总结，承继这一份珍贵的遗产。"习近平总书记也强调："我们决不可抛弃中华民族的优秀文化传统，恰恰相反，我们要很好传承和弘扬，因为这是我们民族的'根'和'魂'，丢了这个'根'和'魂'，就没有根基了。"就在前几天，习近平总书记去考察了河南安阳的殷墟遗址，殷墟出土的甲骨文保存了中国3000年前的文字，从那时到今天，中国的文化传统从未中断过，这在世界上是独一无二的。中国共产党在百年奋斗历程中，始终坚持继承和弘扬中华优秀传统文化。我这里举几个例子。中国共产党的奋斗目标是实现共产主义，这与中国古代哲人曾描绘的大同社会有很多契合的内容，都希望建立一个没有压迫、没有剥削、没有欺诈的理想社会。中国共产党的宗旨是"全心全意为人民服务"，这既是马克思主义"人民创造历史"的唯物史观的体现，也是中国文化传统里"民为邦本""民为贵"思想的延续。中国共产党的思想路线是实事求是，这四个字也是来自中国汉朝的词汇，是中国传统文化的精华。中国共产党人的崇高精神里，很多也继承了中国几千年的文化结晶，本质上是中华优秀传

统文化的内生化延续。比如，自强不息的精神，源自哪里呢？3000年前的《周易》里就有："天行健，君子以自强不息。"不怕牺牲的精神，2300年前的《吕氏春秋》里就有："三军之士，视死如归。"中国共产党外交政策的宗旨是"维护世界和平，促进共同发展"，习近平总书记提出构建人类命运共同体，建设一个"持久和平、普遍安全、共同繁荣、开放包容、清洁美丽的世界"。这个"和平"的"和"字，也是中国文化传统里非常重要的概念。

甲骨文"和"字如下：

龠：一种竹子制作的乐器。

禾：庄稼，粮食。

在中国的语言里，它的意思就是丰衣足食加上载歌载舞，即"和"。

我们希望通过共商共建共享，维护世界和平，构建人类命运共同体，这是中国共产党对中国传统文化的继承和升华。

马克思主义是中国共产党人的理论基石，中国共产党坚持和发展马克思主义，同时坚持马克思主义与中国实际相结合、与中华优秀传统文化相结合。中国共产党人坚信，只有把马克思主义思想精髓同中华优秀传统文化精华贯通起来、同人民群众日用而不觉的共同价值观念融通起来，才能不断赋予科学理论鲜明的中国特色，才能不断夯实马克思主义中国化时代化的历史基础和群众基础，让马克思主义在中国牢牢扎根。一百多年来，中国共产党人激活了中华文化的时代活力，升华了中华思想的时代价值，提升了中华智慧的世界意义，所以我们可以很自豪地说，中国共产党人不愧为中华优秀传统文化的守正创新者。

三、中华文化与世界各种文化可以交流互鉴、取长补短、共同发展

我们主张弘扬中华优秀传统文化，但我们从来不认为只有中华传统文

化才是优秀的。3000多年前,我们的先哲就告诉我们:"学然后知不足""满招损,谦受益",中国文化传统里强调的是从善如流、与时俱进。如果固守自己的传统,完全排斥外来文化,就会造成文化的"贫血",会导致文化的"枯萎"甚至灭亡。世界上各个民族各个国家的文化都有其自身特点,有值得中国学习借鉴的地方。

最近几年,中国很多青年人开始喜欢汉服。汉服是中国古代的服装,是中国文化传统的一部分,但我们不会因为喜欢自己的汉服就拒绝西装,今天会场多数人穿的也是西装。文化传统不同而又不相互冲突,而是共生共长。阳光包含七种色彩,世界也是异彩纷呈。每个国家、每个民族都有自己的历史文化传统,都有自己的长处和优势,应该相互尊重,相互学习,取长补短,共同进步。

谢谢大家!

大力弘扬中华优秀传统文化
不断推进马克思主义中国化时代化

刘荣刚

中央党史和文献研究院第七研究部主任

中共二十大报告指出：中华优秀传统文化源远流长、博大精深，是中华文明的智慧结晶，其中蕴含的天下为公、民为邦本、为政以德、革故鼎新、任人唯贤、天人合一、自强不息、厚德载物、讲信修睦、亲仁善邻等，是中国人民在长期生产生活中积累的宇宙观、天下观、社会观、道德观的重要体现，同科学社会主义价值观主张具有高度契合性。二十大报告不仅阐明了推进马克思主义中国化时代化的路径和方向，而且对正确看待中华优秀传统文化的地位、更好发挥中华优秀传统文化的作用，意义重大。

中华传统文化是以儒、释、道三家为支柱的文化传统。其核心思想文化的形成和发展，大体经历了中国先秦诸子百家争鸣、两汉经学兴盛、魏晋南北朝玄学流行、隋唐儒释道并立、宋明理学发展等几个历史时期。中华传统文化蕴含着丰富的哲学思想、人文精神、教化思想、道德理念，如大道之行、天下为公的大同理想，六合同风、四海一家的大一统传统，民贵君轻、政在养民的民本思想，等贵贱均贫富、损有余补不足的平等观念，法不阿贵、绳不挠曲的正义追求，孝悌忠信、礼义廉耻的道德操守，周虽旧邦、其命维新的改革精神，亲仁善邻、协和万邦的外交之道等。中华优秀传统文化是中华民族的根和脉，既为中华民族生生不息、发展壮大提供了丰厚滋养，也为解决当代人类面临的难题提供了重要启示。

19世纪40年代以来，在中国人民苦苦探寻救国救民道路过程中，中国先进分子以国家兴亡为己任，郑重选择和广泛传播马克思主义真理，激活了中华优秀传统文化的生命力，为推进马克思主义中国化时代化提供了丰富的文化哺育。马克思主义之所以在中国获得普遍信仰，也在于它与中华优秀传统文化存在着天然的一致性。1926年郭沫若发表《马克思进文庙》一文，通过马克思与孔子的想象性对话，阐述了马克思的理想社会和孔子的大同世界不谋而合，展现了马克思主义与儒家思想在一些方面的相通性，在一定程度上解释了马克思主义在中国广泛传播并成为中国共产党人精神支柱的原因所在。

中国共产党既是中华优秀传统文化的忠实传承者和弘扬者，又是中国先进文化的积极倡导者和发展者。党在百年奋斗实践中，不断深化着对中华传统文化的认识。从成立之初对传统文化"激烈地批判"，到新民主主义革命时期"批判地继承"；从社会主义革命和建设时期的"改造和利用"，到改革开放和社会主义现代化建设时期的"传承和弘扬"，再到中国特色社会主义新时代的"创造性转化、创新性发展"，党把马克思主义基本原理同中国具体实际相结合，坚持"取其精华、去其糟粕""百花齐放、百家争鸣""古为今用，推陈出新"等方针，发掘、继承、弘扬中华优秀传统文化精髓，为增强实现中华民族伟大复兴的精神力量、汲取治国理政的理念思维、满足人民日益增长的精神文化需求、培育担当民族复兴大任的时代新人，发挥了重要作用。尤其是以习近平同志为代表的中国共产党人，汲取中华优秀传统文化的思想理念，提出并弘扬和平、发展、公平、正义、民主、自由的全人类共同价值，为推动构建人类命运共同体作出了重要贡献。

习近平总书记指出：中国共产党为什么能，中国特色社会主义为什么好，归根到底是马克思主义行，是中国化时代化的马克思主义行。坚持和发展马克思主义，推进马克思主义中国化时代化，必须坚持把马克思主义基本原理同中国具体实际相结合、同中华优秀传统文化相结合，推动中华优秀传统文化创造性转化、创新性发展，把马克思主义思想精髓同中华优秀传统文化精华贯通起来，同人民群众日用而不觉的共同价值观念融通起来，使中华民族最基本的文化基因与社会主义制度、时代要求适应协调，与当代中国马克思主义、现代生活连接结合，深入挖掘和阐发中华优秀传统文化讲仁爱、重民本、守诚信、崇正义、尚和合、求大同的时代价值，不断创造中华文化新辉煌，不断谱写马克思主义中国化时代化新篇章。

传承中华优秀传统文化
铸牢中华民族共同体意识

傅 琰

新华社研究院研究员

习近平总书记2022年10月28日在河南安阳殷墟遗址考察时说:"中华文明源远流长,从未中断,塑造了我们伟大的民族。"中华优秀传统文化是中华文明的智慧结晶,是中华民族的根与魂。前不久,新华社研究院完成了迎接党的二十大智库课题"铸牢中华民族共同体意识研究"的相关研究工作,"铸牢中华民族共同体意识"是新时代党的民族工作的主线,是马克思主义基本原理同中国具体实际相结合,同中华优秀传统文化相结合的党的重要创新理论。结合学习二十大报告精神,我从中华优秀传统文化对"铸牢中华民族共同体意识"的重大意义谈三点体会。

一、中华优秀传统文化是"中华民族共同体"这一核心概念的文化基因

"中华"是一个古老的名词与概念,是应用于中国这个历史悠久国家具有习惯性意义的通用名号。在中华大地,辽阔的疆域是各民族共同开拓的,悠久的历史是各民族共同书写的,灿烂的文化是各民族共同创造的,伟大的精神是各民族共同培育的。历史上,中国各民族对于以中原王朝为核心的中华政治—文化共同体的认同,不仅表现为对统治君主或所处王朝的认同,还表现为超越朝代的、对历史文化延续性的认同。

1902 年梁启超首次提出"中华民族"。毛泽东在 1939 年发表《中国革命与中国共产党》一文中，明确指出："中国是一个由多数民族结合而成的国家"，但同时又是"一个伟大的民族国家"。这一论断既认同各民族的存在，也认同中华民族作为整体国家民族的概念，是一种双重认同。因而，"中华民族"这一概念包含西方民族理论中"民族"和"族群"两个层级的概念，上层是体现了"一体性"的"中华民族"，下层是体现了内部"多元性"的 56 个"民族"。

"中华民族共同体"是对"中华民族"更为具体的表述，更具有时代意义的延伸。习近平总书记指出："铸牢中华民族共同体意识，就是要引导各族人民牢固树立休戚与共、荣辱与共、生死与共、命运与共的共同体理念。"这是对中华民族大家庭各族同胞共同生活、共同奋斗、共同发展的科学概括和历史总结。"中华民族共同体"这一概念涵盖了中华优秀传统文化的深厚底蕴和文化基因。

二、中华优秀传统文化是铸牢中华民族共同体意识的文化支撑

在几千年的历史中，各族人民相互学习借鉴，相互交融发展，共同创造了悠久灿烂的中华文明。中华优秀传统文化是中华文明的智慧结晶，成为构筑中华民族共有精神家园、铸牢中华民族共同体意识的文化支撑。

中华优秀传统文化中蕴含的关于国家制度和国家治理的丰富思想，是古往今来中华民族大家庭各族同胞对统一多民族国家产生认同的重要思想文化基础，在漫长历史进程中促进了国家统一和稳定，具有历久弥新的时代价值。"大一统"理念便是其中一项重要思想。自 2000 多年前的秦代以来，"大一统"理念始终是中华民族高于一切的政治理念，无论是汉族建立的王朝，还是少数民族建立的王朝，皆以一统天下为己任，都把自己的王朝视为统一多民族国家的正统。这一理念在中华民族多元一体格局的形成中发挥了重要作用，可以说，"大一统"理念是古代中华民族的共同体意识。

中华优秀传统文化是中华民族的精神根脉，铸牢中华民族共同体意识需要依靠中华优秀传统文化的强力支持和持续赋能。根深叶茂，本固枝荣。只有传承和弘扬好中华优秀传统文化，中华民族共同体才能牢不可破，民族团结进步之花才能长盛不衰。

三、中华优秀传统文化的创造性转化、创新性发展为铸牢中华民族共同体意识凝聚起强大的文化自信

中华优秀传统文化的宇宙观、天下观、社会观、道德观深邃而智慧，具有跨越时空的永恒魅力，同时，中华优秀传统文化中的具体内容必须与时代精神相结合，与现代社会相协调，才能推进文化自信自强，汇聚起实现民族复兴的磅礴力量。

中华文化是各民族文化的集大成，各民族文化是中华文化的组成部分。习近平总书记非常重视少数民族传统文化的创新传承，他指出，要弘扬和保护各民族传统文化，去粗取精、推陈出新，努力实现创造性转化和创新性发展。进入新时代的十年来，中国少数民族文学发展工程、中国少数民族电影工程、少数民族古籍保护工作陆续启动，少数民族文化传承、文艺创作、产业发展迎来"黄金期"，在国家的重视和保护下，重新焕发生机、迸发活力，铸就中华文化新辉煌。

例如，"格萨尔"是一部融汇了中国藏族、蒙古族等少数民族传统文化、社会、经济、道德和习俗等知识体系的"百科全书"式的伟大史诗。几十年来，中国政府除了投入大量资金开展抢救性保护工作之外，还于2022年创作了动画电影《格萨尔王之磨炼》，将"格萨尔"搬上了大银幕，使得这部英雄史诗以更多元、更新颖的方式被传颂和弘扬。

中华优秀传统文化的创造性转化、创新性发展巩固了全党全国各族人民团结奋斗的共同思想基础，凝聚起铸牢中华民族共同体意识的强大文化自信，推动各族人民不断迈向社会主义现代化强国！

二十大报告中的中华优秀传统文化

安　吉

中央党史和文献研究院外国专家（俄文）

刚刚闭幕的中国共产党第二十次全国代表大会不仅是中国人民政治生活中的一件大事，同时它也引发了全世界的关注，能够作为外国专家参与其中，我深感荣幸。

最近，我在很多媒体平台上都看到了俄罗斯网友对二十大的讨论，除了中国式现代化、绿色低碳发展、科技创新等话题以外，文化自信自强也被俄罗斯网友广泛讨论。在我参与二十大报告的翻译过程中，报告中关于中国传统文化的很多表述都给我留下了深刻的印象。报告中说，要开辟马克思主义中国化时代化新境界，必须做到两个结合，一是要与中国具体实际相结合。只有与时俱进，一切从实际出发，着眼于解决新时代改革开放和社会主义现代化建设中出现的实际问题，才能做出符合中国实际和时代要求的正确回答。二是要与中国传统文化相结合。马克思主义是党和国家的指导思想，中华优秀传统文化是中华民族的精神命脉。中华文化历史悠久、博大精深，融汇了五千多年来中国人民的智慧结晶。仔细研读报告，会发现很多中国传统文化思想都贯穿于国家各项政策当中，比如"天下为公""民为邦本"的思想与中国共产党"执政为民、立党为公"的理念息息相关。"天人合一"的传统思想造就了中国共产党"人与自然和谐相处"的执政理念。在中国共产党干部选拔标准中我们又可以看到"任人唯贤"这一中国传统思想的影子。找到中国传统文化与中国共产党执政理念之间的这种联系，让我更加深刻地体会到"守正创新"的真正意义。中国共产党和中国人民正是在传承中华优秀传统文化的基础上进行创造性转化和创新性发展,才让中国文化繁荣发展,同时又指导了中国的改革和发展实践。

"讲信修睦""亲仁善邻"是中国外交理念的重要体现。当前,中国积极深入参与全球治理、向全世界提出更多围绕国际治理的新概念、倡议和合作项目,为国际社会提供中国智慧、中国方案、中国力量。

接下来,我想具体阐述国际上被各个国家广为推崇的"人类命运共同体"的概念以及很多国家广泛参与的共建"一带一路"倡议。这两个都是中华优秀传统文化的结晶,反映了全人类的共同价值追求以及中国人民和世界各国人民的共同利益诉求。"命运共同体"的概念体现了中国传统文化的重要思想,如"和衷共济""和合共生""协和万邦"。而"一带一路"倡议则是中国坚持推动构建人类命运共同体的生动实践。从古代的丝绸之路到新时代的"一带一路",中国毫不动摇秉持互利共赢的对外交往传统,这一倡议能为世界持久和平与共同繁荣作出重要贡献。

对于二十大报告的翻译来说,如何将这些中国传统文化的精髓用俄罗斯人听得懂的语言表达出来也就成了我们工作的重点和难点。翻译过程中,我们既考虑了这些成语本身的含义,又兼顾了译文在具体语境中的具体所指和文章的可读性,让我们的译文成为连接中国古代和现代,成为连接中国和世界的纽带和桥梁。中国传统文化不仅是中国人民的宝贵财富,也深刻影响着全世界。

中共二十大的文化与发展

德拉加娜·米特罗维奇

塞尔维亚贝尔格莱德大学政治学部亚洲研究所主任

建立在世界最古老文明基础上的中华人民共和国，是中华传统文化在各个层面上的代表。全体中国人民也都受到中华文化的浸润，从家庭日常生活、基层社区和各级政府行为准则，到商业、产业、设计、语言、饮食和习惯，以及价值观和传统习俗，都深受独特中华文化的影响。它是中国自信自强的来源，是中国过去和现在能够取得令人骄傲的成就的源泉。

中国的发展模式深深植根于它的文化和传统。

中共二十大提出的中国发展战略在很大程度上来源于中华文化及其悠久传统。中国共产党的发展方式是承诺以人民为中心并致力于实现"共同发展"的高质量发展。这种发展道路源于团结协作、胸怀天下的中国传统价值观。

中国实现了消除绝对贫困的目标，这不仅是中国人自古以来的梦想，也是当代中国梦的一部分。中国在改革开放中成功实现了使亿万人民摆脱贫困的宏伟目标。中国在推进中国式现代化以及城市化过程中实施的发展战略是以长期高质量发展为目标的，这是其根植于传统文化的又一例证。

共同发展是中国向全球伙伴提供的一种发展路径，主要通过全球公共产品与合作平台，如"一带一路"倡议来实现。为实现开放和更高质量的互联互通，中国正致力于建立一个新的全球发展治理模式，并倡导真正的多边主义，其中蕴含的文化内核正是传统文化对和谐与和平的追求。一方面，中国传统文化强调尊重其他文化，这是基于儒家关于通过仁爱创造一个多元文化世界的理念。另一方面，中国传统文化提倡和而不同的和谐理念，既为包容文化差异提供空间，也决不把自己的观念强加于人。中国通过道德和共同进步而非冲突对抗来推广中国文化及其整体影响力。同时，中国也呼吁全球伙伴加强对话协商，创造一个为各方提供发展机遇的新型多极世界。

Speech at the Opening Ceremony of the "Hong Ting Forum: Understanding the 20th CPC National Congress" Seminar

Qu Qingshan

President of the Institute of Party History and Literature of the
CPC Central Committee, Chairman of the National High-Level
Think Tank Council of the Institute of Party History and Literature
of the CPC Central Committee

Distinguished Representatives and Guests,
Ladies and Gentlemen,
Dear Friends,

Good afternoon. Today, ambassadors and other diplomatic envoys to China from almost 80 countries, think tank experts, and journalists, as well as representatives from China's central departments, national high-end think tanks, and central media groups gather both in-person and online to attend the inaugural Hong Ting Forum. Together, we will conduct in-depth discussions with a focus on the new concepts, frameworks, and formulations put forward at the 20th National Congress of the Communist Party of China (CPC). First, on behalf of the Party History and Literature Institute of the CPC Central Committee, I would like to express a warm welcome to all guests attending the forum.

Ten days ago, the 20th CPC National Congress came to a successful conclusion in Beijing. The Congress was a meeting of great importance, taking place at a critical time as the entire Party and the Chinese people of all ethnic groups embark on a new journey to build China into a modern socialist country in all respects and advance toward the Second Centenary Goal. In his report to the Congress, General Secretary Xi Jinping comprehensively reviewed the work of the past five years and the great changes in the first decade of the new era, defined the CPC's missions and tasks for the new journey of the new era, and set forth the development goals and major policies of the Party and the state for the next five years and beyond. As two of China's national high-end think tanks, the Institute of Party History and Literature of the CPC Central Committee and Xinhua News Agency have joined hands to host this forum under the theme of "Understanding the 20th CPC National Congress." We hope to provide an effective platform for communication and exchange that will help the international community in gaining an in-depth and timely understanding of the CPC's vision and propositions.

Today, I would like to take this opportunity to share with you my understanding of the guiding principles of the Congress.

First, the CPC is a strong leadership force for promoting national rejuvenation on all fronts. As the report to the Congress states, "Our Party has a pivotal role in building China into a modern socialist country in all respects and in advancing the rejuvenation of the Chinese nation on all fronts."

The CPC is dedicated to pursuing happiness for the Chinese people and rejuvenation for the Chinese nation. It is also dedicated to human progress and world harmony. Over the past one hundred years, the CPC has remained true to its original aspiration and founding mission and determinedly forged ahead. In the first decade of the new era, in particular, the Party has, under the strong leadership of the Central Committee with Comrade Xi Jinping at its core, firmly devoted itself to carrying out its founding mission and has led the Chinese nation in driving the great transformation from standing up and growing prosperous to becoming strong.

Generation after generation, Chinese Communists have always adhered to a people-centered philosophy, always put the people first, and always worked relentlessly to meet the people's aspirations for a better life. We are fully aware that when the people enjoy better lives, their wholehearted and firm support for our Party will be even more extensive. The support of over a billion Chinese people is our Party's greatest source of confidence in exercising long-term governance.

Of course, as a party exercising long-term governance in a major country, the CPC is sure to face complicated and volatile circumstances, and it must always be prepared to face sterner risks and challenges. Therefore, it must tirelessly pursue self-reform and self-improvement to keep enhancing its governance abilities and maintain its advanced nature and integrity. Only by doing so, can the CPC better unite and lead the Chinese people in shouldering their mission.

Second, promoting national rejuvenation through the path of Chinese modernization is the mission and task of the CPC on its new journey in the new era. The report to the Congress states that "From this day forward, the central task of the Communist Party of China will be to lead the Chinese people of all ethnic groups in a concerted effort to realize the Second Centenary Goal of building China into a great modern socialist country in all respects and to advance the rejuvenation of the Chinese nation on all fronts through the path of Chinese modernization."

Modernization is a common pursuit of the peoples of all countries. Based on decades of exploration and practice since the founding of the People's Republic of China in 1949, especially since the launch of reform and opening up in 1978, as well as the new breakthroughs made in theory and practice since the 18th National Congress, the CPC has succeeded in advancing and expanding Chinese modernization. It contains elements that are common to the modernization processes of all countries, but it is more characterized by features that are unique to the Chinese context. These unique features are a huge population, common prosperity for all, coordinated material and cultural-ethical advancement, harmony between humanity and nature, and a peaceful development path.

Here, I would like to place emphasis on the path of peaceful development through which Chinese modernization will be achieved. China will not tread the old path of war, colonization, and plunder taken by some countries. On the contrary, we are committed to pursuing shared development with all other countries in accordance with the principles of mutual respect and equitable cooperation. China will work with countries around the world to promote humanity's shared values of peace, development, fairness, justice, democracy, and freedom; strive to create new opportunities for the world with its own development; and continue working to build a human community with a shared future and create a new form of human advancement. In doing so, China will provide humanity with more Chinese insight, better Chinese input, and greater Chinese strength to help solve the common problem facing humanity regarding the path to modernization.

Third, fine traditional Chinese culture has provided strong support for advancing the rejuvenation of the Chinese nation on all fronts. The report to the 20th CPC National Congress points out that "With a history stretching back to antiquity, China's fine traditional culture is extensive and profound; it is the crystallization of the wisdom of Chinese civilization... and highly consistent with the values and propositions of scientific socialism."

The Chinese nation could not have maintained continuous growth and development or have emerged stronger from many setbacks it endured without the rich nourishment and powerful support of Chinese culture. China's fine traditional culture represents the very root and soul of the Chinese nation. It is this profound heritage that enables the CPC to stay confident in our history and culture and to maintain a firm footing amidst global cultural interaction.

The CPC is a party that was born and grew strong on Chinese soil. Outstanding Chinese culture, therefore, naturally runs in its blood. Chinese Communists have always worked to faithfully preserve and carry forward China's fine traditional culture.

Chinese culture holds that a just cause should be pursued for the common good; that the people are the foundation of the state and that the government should protect the people; that the diplomatic principles of good neighborliness and harmony should be respected in relations with all countries; and that harmony is precious and that warlike nations will eventually perish. China's fine traditional political culture and governance wisdom have provided our Party with a profound historical heritage, important cultural nourishment, and powerful inspiration for its successful governance practices.

Chinese culture has much in common with the rich and diverse cultures of other countries. Through intercultural exchanges, learning, and interactions, China's fine traditional culture will undoubtedly be able to work in tandem with the outstanding cultures created by the peoples of other countries to provide the right cultural compass for humanity.

Ladies and Gentlemen,

Friends,

At present, momentous changes of a like not seen in a century are accelerating across the world. In the face of a complex international environment, countries around the world need to further strengthen exchanges and cooperation, jointly promote the building of a human community with a shared future, and work together to address various risks and challenges.

Our institute assumes the important responsibilities of building a comprehensive system of theoretical research for the CPC, of creating a high-end research platform for the Party's history and theories, and of developing a reliable repository of literature, reservoir of ideas, and think tank for the CPC Central Committee. Xinhua News Agency is China's national news agency and a world-class media group.

Going forward, our two high-end think tanks will continue working together to provide dialogue platforms to facilitate the international community in gaining a deeper understanding of the new historical and theoretical concepts, frameworks, and formulations of the Party in the form of think tank forums. We are willing to work with think tank experts and friends from the media to further strengthen exchanges and mutual learning, so that the world can better understand China, the Chinese people, and the Communist Party of China.

We hope that everyone will engage in in-depth discussions and exchanges around the theme of this forum in order to foster wisdom, stimulate ideas, and build consensus.

Finally, I would like to wish this forum every success.

Thank you.

Speech at "Hong Ting Forum: Understanding the 20th CPC National Congress" Seminar

Fu Hua

President of Xinhua News Agency, Director of the
Academic Committee of New China Research, Xinhua News Agency

Distinguished President Qu Qingshan,
Dear Guests,
Ladies and Gentlemen,
Friends,

Good afternoon. It's a great pleasure to meet you at the Museum of the Communist Party of China. The 20th National Congress of the Communist Party of China concluded not long ago. Thus, it is of special significance for us to hold the "Hong Ting Forum: Understanding the 20th CPC National Congress" Seminar today at the exhibition hall showing the centennial history of the Party.

The 20th National Congress of the Communist Party of China is a meeting of great importance. It was convened at a critical time as the entire Party and the Chinese people of all ethnic groups embark on a new journey to build China into a modern socialist country in all respects and advance towards the Second Centenary Goal. The report presented by General Secretary Xi Jinping serves as a political declaration and a program of action for the Party to rally and lead the Chinese people of all ethnic groups in securing new victories for socialism with Chinese characteristics and provides a window of thought and a cultural identity for the world to understand China.

The 20th CPC National Congress commanded the attention of the world in recent days, and Xinhua News Agency interviewed many international figures. They said the 20th CPC National Congress is a milestone, which not only has a far-reaching impact on China but also injects impetus into countries around the world to jointly address challenges and achieve common development. They thought CPC has pioneered a new development path of China in the past century, and the Congress will profoundly impact China's future development. The interviewees expected the Party to make greater contributions to the world from a new historical starting point. These voices reflected that the international community speaks highly of and hopes to understand the visions outlined at the 20th CPC National Congress.

To better introduce the 20th CPC National Congress and respond to the concerns of the international community, Xinhua News Agency and the Institute of Party History and Literature of the CPC Central Committee co-hosted the seminar. With the three topics, "Key Role of the CPC," "Chinese Modernization," and "China's Fine Traditional Culture," we try to demonstrate the major achievements and significance of the 20th CPC National Congress through in-depth discussions and exchanges and help the international community better understand the Party's governance concepts and strategies.

—To understand the 20th CPC National Congress, we should first recognize the power of truth in the Party's new theories. At the fundamental level, we owe the success of our Party and socialism with Chinese characteristics to the fact that Marxism works, particularly when it is adapted to the Chinese context and the needs of our times. Xi Jinping Thought on Socialism with Chinese Characteristics for a New Era is the Marxism of contemporary China and of the 21st century and embodies the best Chinese culture and ethos of this era, thus achieving a new breakthrough in adapting Marxism to the Chinese context and the needs of the times. China's truly momentous and extraordinary achievements in the past five years and the great changes in the first decade of the new era have fully demonstrated the strong power of truth and great significance in practice of Xi Jinping Thought on Socialism with Chinese Characteristics for a New Era. The Thought integrates basic tenets of Marxism with China's specific realities and fine traditional culture, keeps responding to the questions posed by China, by the world, by the people, and by the times, and draws extensively from the fine traditional Chinese culture, to ensure that Marxism puts down deep roots in China and scientific socialism brims with renewed vitality in 21st-century China.

—**To understand the 20th CPC National Congress, we must recognize the Party's distinctive character of maintaining self-confident and self-reliant.** One point underpinning the CPC's successes over the past century is that China's issues must be dealt with by Chinese people in light of the Chinese context. Only by taking root in the rich historical and cultural soil of the country and the nation can the truth of Marxism flourish here in China. The 20th CPC National Congress proposed missions and tasks of the Party on the new journey of the new era, and defined Chinese modernization as the approach to advancing the rejuvenation of the Chinese nation on all fronts. Chinese modernization is socialist modernization pursued under the leadership of the Communist Party of China. It contains elements that are common to the modernization processes of all countries, but it is more characterized by features that are unique to the Chinese context. There is no fixed model for modernization; and there is no single standard for modernization that fits all. Chinese modernization broadens the path towards modernization for developing countries and provides a Chinese solution in mankind's search for a better social system.

—**To understand the 20th CPC National Congress, we must recognize the Party's global vision.** The Communist Party of China is dedicated to pursuing happiness for the Chinese people and rejuvenation for the Chinese nation. It is also dedicated to human progress and world harmony. Over the past decade, China has unswervingly followed the path of peaceful development, contributed to the building of a human community with a shared future, promoted humanity's shared values, worked to foster a new type of international relations, stood firm in protecting international fairness and justice, and advocated and practiced true multilateralism. China has continued its efforts to safeguard world peace, contribute to global development, and uphold international order, which comprehensively displays the Party's commitment to maintaining a global vision. Today, our world, our times, and history are changing in ways like never before. The world is undergoing accelerating changes unseen in a century, it has entered a new phase of turbulence and change, and it has once again reached a crossroads in history. This requires us to jointly take on the responsibility for maintaining peace, follow the path of peaceful development, keep moving towards the goal of building a human community with a shared future, and work together to create a better future for mankind.

Ladies and Gentlemen,

Friends,

Xinhua News Agency is the official state news agency of China with international influence, acting to bridge China and the rest of the world. We will keep innovating our international communication capacity and tell well the stories of China, of the CPC, and of the new era we are living in in a more friendly and authentic manner, giving full play to our role as a "bridge of communication."

Xinhua News Agency and the Institute of Party History and Literature of the CPC Central Committee are both leaders in our respective fields and have long maintained a close partnership. I hope that we can take this seminar as an opportunity to intensify exchanges, deepen practical cooperation, tap into our strengths, and make greater contributions to China's development and human progress.

Guests present are encouraged to have in-depth discussions, share insights, and inspire one another. I also hope that today's event can help you develop a better understanding of the 20th CPC National Congress, of the Party, and of the Chinese people. Let us work together to bring the country and the world into a new stage of integrated growth.

To conclude, I wish the seminar a full success. Thank you.

The Key Role of the Communist Party of China

CPC Is Pivotal to China's Success

Huang Yibing

Vice President of the Institute of Party History and Literature of the CPC Central Committee, Vice Chairman of the National High-Level Think Tank Council of the Institute of Party History and Literature of the CPC Central Committee

The report to the 20th National Congress of the CPC pointed out that our Party has a pivotal role in building China into a modern socialist country in all respects and in advancing the rejuvenation of the Chinese nation on all fronts. This important statement reveals the Party's position as the leadership core in the cause of socialism with Chinese characteristics in the new era.

The CPC's pivotal role is an important guarantee of our success in the past, and it is also a fundamental guidance for us to continue to succeed in the future. I would like to stress four points regarding this topic.

First, establishing the Party's pivotal role is a lesson drawn from history. To understand China, we must understand the Communist Party of China. Since the very day of its founding, the Party has made seeking happiness for the Chinese people and rejuvenation for the Chinese nation its aspiration and mission. Over the past century, by focusing on the historic goal of realizing the great rejuvenation of the Chinese nation, Chinese Communists have concerned themselves with the future of the country and the nation and sacrificed themselves for greater good. Through unregretful devotion and sacrifices, they have made selfless and courageous efforts to perform great feats. Their pursuit of truth and sense of responsibility are like shining stars on China's path to national rejuvenation, illuminating the skies of the Chinese nation which used to be desperately dark. As Mao Zedong confidently stated, "The Chinese people will see that, once China's destiny is in the hands of the people, China, like the sun rising in the east, will illuminate every corner of the land with a brilliant flame, swiftly clean up the mire left by the reactionary government, heal the wounds of war and build a new, powerful and prosperous people's republic worthy of the name."

Over the past century, the Party's tenacious endeavors have fundamentally changed the future of the Chinese people. Freed from bullying, oppression, and subjugation, the Chinese people have become the masters of the country, of society, and of their own fate, and people's democracy has developed steadily. The more than 1.4 billion Chinese people have achieved moderate prosperity in all respects, and are now seeing their aspirations for a better life become a reality. The Party's tenacious endeavors have opened up the right path for achieving national rejuvenation. China has moved from a state of disunity and division to a high level of unity and solidarity, from weakness and poverty to strength and moderate prosperity in all respects, and from being beaten and bullied to becoming independent, self-reliant, and confident. China has completed a process of industrialization that took developed countries several centuries in the space of mere decades, bringing about the two miracles of rapid economic growth and enduring social stability. The Party's tenacious endeavors have demonstrated the strong vitality of Marxism. The Party has rallied under the banner of Marxism, continued to adapt Marxism to the Chinese context and the needs of our times while using such theories to guide China's ongoing social transformation, and embraced all the outstanding achievements of human society with an open mind. The Party's tenacious endeavors have had a profound influence on the course of world history. The Party has led the people in pioneering a Chinese path to modernization, creating a new model for human advancement and becoming an important driving force for human development and progress. The Party's tenacious endeavors have made it a forerunner of the times. The Party has remained true to its nature and purpose, upheld its ideals and convictions, and stayed committed to its founding mission. It has developed a long line of inspiring principles originating from its great founding spirit. Through painstaking efforts, it has found an answer to the question of how to escape the historical cycle of rise and fall. The answer is self-reform. Such efforts have ensured that the Party will never change its nature, its conviction, or its character.

Second, establishing the Party's pivotal role is a solemn choice made by the people. The Communist Party of China is a party for the people. Between 1921 and 1949, in the CPC-led revolutionary ranks, more than 3.7 million martyrs laid down their lives for the interests of the people—this only included those who could be identified by name. In the period of peaceful development, Party members have risen to the occasion wherever difficulties and dangers exist in response to earthquakes, floods, and other emergencies. In the battle against poverty, more than 1,800 Party members and officials have made the ultimate sacrifice. Since the Covid-19 outbreak, nearly 400 Party members and officials have given their lives in responding to the pandemic. The Party represents the fundamental interests of the overwhelming majority of the Chinese people. It has no special interests of its own, nor has it ever represented the interests of any particular interest group, any power group, or any privileged stratum. It has always served the people wholeheartedly and put the people first, making continued efforts to benefit the people.

Under the leadership of the Party, the Chinese people today are more self-confident, self-reliant, and capable of self-improvement. They have greater ambition, fortitude, and determination, and they are exhibiting historic initiative and creativity as never seen before. Today, China's per capita GDP has topped 10,000 US dollars, and China boasts the world's largest middle-income group and the world's largest social security system. It has thriving cosmopolitan cities, beautiful and harmonious countryside, a dynamic market, and a stable and orderly society. Through its tenacious endeavors, the Party aims to give the people a greater sense of fulfillment and happiness and to achieve common prosperity through development and progress.

Third, establishing the Party's pivotal role demonstrates its strong sense of mission. Among all political parties in modern China, the Communist Party of China was the first to put forward the goal of realizing national rejuvenation, and the first to elaborate on the historical mission and tasks for national rejuvenation; and it has made persistent efforts to achieve this goal.

By leading the people to great success in the new-democratic revolution, the Party has created fundamental social conditions for realizing national rejuvenation. By leading the people to great success in socialist revolution and construction, the Party has laid fundamental political prerequisites and institutional basis for realizing national rejuvenation. By leading the people to great success in reform, opening up, and socialist modernization, the Party has created new, vibrant institutions and material conditions for realizing national rejuvenation.

The new era has marked three major events of great immediate importance and profound historical significance for the cause of the Party and the people: We embraced the centenary of the Communist Party of China; we ushered in a new era of socialism with Chinese characteristics; and we eradicated absolute poverty and finished building a moderately prosperous society in all respects, thus completing the First Centenary Goal. These were historic feats—feats accomplished by the Communist Party of China and the Chinese people striving in unity, feats that will be forever recorded in the Chinese nation's history, and feats that will profoundly influence the world. Over the past decade of the new era, we have fully implemented the Party's basic theory, line, and policy, adopted a number of strategic measures, developed a range of transformative practices, and made a series of breakthroughs and landmark advances. We have withstood risks, challenges, and trials in the political, economic, ideological, and natural domains, secured historic achievements and seen historic changes in the cause of the Party and the country, and taken China on a new journey toward building a modern socialist country in all respects. The Chinese nation has achieved the great transformation from standing up and growing prosperous to becoming strong. The rejuvenation of the Chinese nation is now on an irreversible historical course. Today, we are closer, more confident, and more capable than ever of reaching the goal of rejuvenating the Chinese nation.

Fourth, establishing the Party's pivotal role reflects its sober-mindedness and determination. The CPC was born amid domestic turmoil and foreign aggression, was tempered through numerous tribulations, and has grown strong by overcoming risks and challenges. In this course, it has always been mindful of risks and potential dangers. Under the new circumstances and facing new tasks, General Secretary Xi Jinping has told all Party members to stay true to the Party's founding mission, to remain modest, prudent, and hard-working, to have the courage and ability to carry on our fight, and to remain confident in our history and exhibit greater historical initiative. This reminds us of Mao Zedong's remarks on the eve of the countrywide victory in the Chinese revolution: "To win countrywide victory is only the first step in a long march of ten thousand *li*. Even if this step is worthy of pride, it is comparatively tiny... the road after the revolution will be longer, the work greater and more arduous. This must be made clear now in the Party."

Today, we may also say that what's past is prologue as we pursue lasting greatness for the Chinese nation. We will encounter even more risks and challenges and fierce storms ahead. General Secretary Xi Jinping has pointed out, "As the largest Marxist governing party in the world, we must always stay alert and determined to tackle the special challenges that a large party like ours faces, so as to maintain the people's support and consolidate our position as the long-term governing party. All of us in the Party must bear in mind that full and rigorous self-governance is an unceasing endeavor and that self-reform is a journey to which there is no end. We must never slacken our efforts and never allow ourselves to become weary or beaten. We must persevere with full and rigorous self-governance, continue to advance the great new project of Party building in the new era, and use our own transformation to steer social transformation. Only by pressing ahead with unwavering commitment and perseverance will we be able to answer the call of our times and meet the expectations of our people. "

The Chinese people are fully aware of the fact that the great transformation in the past ten years of the new era are fundamentally attributable to General Secretary Xi Jinping steering our course as the core of the Party Central Committee and of the Party as a whole as well as the sound guidance of Xi Jinping Thought on Socialism with Chinese Characteristics for a New Era. The Chinese people is convinced that, on the new journey ahead, we will definitely be able to open new ground for advancing the cause of the Party and the country if we do the following: thoroughly understanding the decisive significance of the establishment of both Comrade Xi Jinping's core position on the Party Central Committee and in the Party as a whole and the guiding role of Xi Jinping Thought on Socialism with Chinese Characteristics for a New Era; remaining focused on the country's most fundamental interests; boosting our consciousness of the need to maintain political integrity, think in big-picture terms, follow the leadership core, and keep in alignment with the central Party leadership; staying confident in the path, the theory, the system, and the culture of socialism with Chinese characteristics; firmly upholding Comrade Xi Jinping's core position on the Party Central Committee and in the Party as a whole and upholding the Central Committee's authority and its centralized, unified leadership; and seeing that Party leadership is exercised in all aspects and every stage of the endeavors of the Party and the country. The vibrant CPC has made spectacular achievements through its great endeavors over the past century, and our new endeavors will surely lead to more spectacular achievements.

Pivotal Role of the CPC in Building China into a Modern Socialist Country in All Respects
—An Important Perspective to Understand the Guiding Principles of the 20th CPC National Congress

Zhang Hefu

First-Class Inspector of the First Research Department of the Institute of Party History and Literature of the CPC Central Committee

In the report to the 20th National Congress of the Communist Party of China, General Secretary Xi Jinping stressed, "Our Party has a pivotal role in building China into a modern socialist country in all respects and in advancing the rejuvenation of the Chinese nation on all fronts." His statement carries profound meaning and is of great importance for understanding the guiding principles of the 20th CPC National Congress. In my opinion, we can grasp its concrete meaning from the following three aspects.

1. The great achievements and the great changes in the first decade of the new era hinges on the leadership of the CPC. Over the course of a century of endeavor, the Communist Party of China has tempered itself and grown stronger. It has grown better at providing political leadership, giving theoretical guidance, inspiring society, and organizing the people. In the past decade of the new era, the Communist Party of China has withstood risks, challenges, and trials in the political, economic, ideological, and natural domains, won the largest battle against poverty in human history as scheduled, and achieved moderate prosperity which had been the millennia-old dream of the Chinese nation. As a result, we have secured historic achievements and seen historic changes in the cause of socialism with Chinese characteristics, and taken China on a new journey toward building a modern socialist country in all respects. All these achievements, more than anything else, are attributable to the strong leadership of the Communist Party of China as it exercises overall leadership and coordinates the efforts of all sides, to General Secretary Xi Jinping at the core of both the CPC Central Committee and the entire Party who takes the helm and charts the course, and to the sound guidance of Xi Jinping Thought on Socialism with Chinese Characteristics for a New Era. The most important achievement of the 20th CPC National Congress is the election of a new central leadership with Comrade Xi Jinping at its core. With General Secretary Xi continuing to act as the navigator and helmsman, the great ship of China will resolutely advance in the right direction, catch the wind, cut through the waves, and fulfill the development strategies and objectives formulated at the Congress.

2. The key to building China into a great modern socialist country in all respects lies on the leadership of the CPC. It is noted in the report to the 20th National Congress that, "From this day forward, the central task of the Communist Party of China will be to lead the Chinese people of all ethnic groups in a concerted effort to realize the Second Centenary Goal of building China into a great modern socialist country in all respects and to advance the rejuvenation of the Chinese nation on all fronts through a Chinese path to modernization." It is also stressed that, "Chinese modernization is socialist modernization pursued under the leadership of the Communist Party of China." The report elaborated the essential requirements of Chinese modernization, the most important of which is "upholding the leadership of the Communist Party of China." These statements offered a clear explanation of the defining feature and the greatest strength of Chinese modernization. The Party has always represented the fundamental interests of all Chinese people; it stands with them through thick and thin and shares a common fate with them. The Party has no special interests of its own—it has never represented any individual interest group, power group, or privileged stratum. This has enabled it to constantly demonstrate its advanced nature and integrity in practice, to rally the overwhelming majority of the people to make one remarkable achievement after another, to pioneer a distinctively Chinese path to modernization, and to create a new model for human advancement. In the face of a more complicated environment and higher requirements, we must and can only uphold the leadership of the CPC in building China into a great modern socialist country in all respects.

3. To build China into a great modern socialist country in all respects, we must make the Party stronger and ensure that the Party exercises effective self-supervision and full and rigorous self-governance. Focusing on exercising full and rigorous self-governance and advancing the great new project of Party building in the new era, seven requirements has been put forth in the report to the 20th National Congress, demonstrating the Party's attitude and determination in tackling the special challenges it faces. They are as follows: 1) upholding and strengthening the centralized, unified leadership of the Party Central Committee to ensure the implementation of its major decisions and plans as well as the Party's solidarity and unity; 2) enhancing ideological and understanding level and the ability to make decisions and solve problems with Xi Jinping Thought on Socialism with Chinese Characteristics for a New Era, and turning this latest theoretical innovation of the Party into a powerful force for strengthening ideals, enhancing Party consciousness, guiding practice, and advancing our work; 3) improving the systems and regulations for the Party's self-reform, running the Party with systems and regulations, and making Party building more effective; 4) cultivating officials capable of shouldering the mission of national rejuvenation to ensure that we have qualified successors to carry forward our cause; 5) enhancing the political and organizational functions of Party organizations to fully exerting the Party's advantages and strength; 6) taking strict steps to improve Party conduct and enforce Party discipline, so as to ensure that all Party members, especially officials, can strictly discipline themselves and take responsibilities; and 7) winning the tough and protracted battle against corruption, eradicating the tumors endangering the health of our Party, and carrying out the most thorough kind of self-reform in accordance with Party's nature, purpose, and goals. Taking aim at building China into a great modern socialist country in all respects, the CPC put forward these requirements to address problems within the Party. These requirements embody the Party's willingness to learn from history and its commitment to remaining firmly grounded in the present while setting sights on the future. They are of pivotal importance for the CPC in preserving its advanced nature and integrity and strengthening its governance capacity as it leads China's modernization drive.

History and the People Have Chosen the Communist Party of China

Zhang Xudong

Vice Director of Internal News Editorial Department of Xinhua News Agency

President Huang,

Distinguished Guests,

Greetings to you all.

I'm glad to have the opportunity to share my views. As a special researcher at Xinhua Institute and a reporter, I covered the 20th National Congress of the Communist Party of China. More than 2,300 delegates and specially invited delegates attending the congress have been placed in great trust of more than 96 million Party members and earnest expectations of more than 1.4 billion people. The Chinese people all know that China's success hinges on the Party; by following the Party, there is nothing we cannot accomplish.

Following the Party, the Chinese people in their hundreds of millions have become better off. This country is its people; the people are the country. In the report to the 20th CPC National Congress, General Secretary Xi Jinping noted that "As the Communist Party of China has led the people in fighting to establish and develop the People's Republic, it has really been fighting for their support." Those words reveal the mystery why the CPC has won the support of the people and why the people have always followed the Party.

Pei Chunliang, 52, is one of the delegates to the 20th CPC National

Congress. He serves as the Party Branch Secretary of Peizhai Village, Huixian City, Henan Province, which was a provincially designated poverty-stricken village in the foothills of the Taihang Mountains. Since the 18th CPC National Congress in 2012, Pei and the villager committee have set up Party groups in various fields such as agriculture, industry, and commerce, and the villagers' annual per capita income has increased several times. Pei epitomizes millions of Party members working in local communities who lead the people toward prosperity.

On the day of its founding in 1921, the CPC identified as its founding mission the pursuit of happiness for the Chinese people and rejuvenation for the Chinese nation. The Chinese people, once denigrated as the "sick man of East Asia," now enjoy the largest social safety net in the world. China's average life expectancy has risen to 78 years from 35 years when the People's Republic of China was founded in 1949. In the great changes over the past 10 years of the new era, a total of 255,000 work teams and more than 3 million first secretaries and officials have been assigned to villages nationwide, where they worked to eradicate poverty. Among them, more than 1,800 have lost their lives for the cause of poverty alleviation. After eight years of arduous endeavors, we have won the largest battle against poverty in human history. With nearly 100 million rural residents being lifted out of poverty, the Chinese people have attained the goal of building a moderately prosperous society in all respects.

The CPC is a party of the people. The CPC's fundamental purpose of serving people wholeheartedly was first written into the Party Constitution during the Seventh CPC National Congress held in 1945. From "serving the people" to "a people-centered philosophy," the CPC has always put the people first in everything it does and made every effort to secure good results for the people. Now starting from a higher historical starting point in development, the CPC has further highlighted achieving common prosperity for all. Guided by the report to the 20th CPC National Congress, the Chinese people are striding forward on a new journey of building a modern socialist country in all respects.

Following the Party, the ancient nation of China has embarked on the path to national rejuvenation. One month before the 20th CPC National Congress, I had an opportunity to conduct an interview at the site of the First CPC National Congress in Shanghai. About one hundred years ago, the Chinese people were struggling with an indomitable spirit amid repeated setbacks to save the nation from subjugation. In 1929, an article titled Ten Questions about the Future of China was published in Shanghai-based *Life Weekly*, which asked, "When will our country's production of grain be self-sufficient with no fear of famine? When will our country be able to produce pens, lampshades, watches, and cars for our people? ..." All these are full of the Chinese people's expectations: "When we can give positive answers to the ten questions, China will be prosperous and strong."

The past hundred years have witnessed profound and transformative changes in China. Now it ranks first in terms of the grain output, the manufacturing sector, the trade in goods.... Under the leadership of the CPC, China is brimming with vitality, and has created and is creating miracle upon miracle that will go down in history.

I also covered the 18th and 19th CPC national congresses, and I can truly feel the big strides China is making in the new era. The great changes in the past decade of the new era have provided better institutional conditions, stronger material foundations, and a source of inspiration for realizing national rejuvenation. The rejuvenation of the Chinese nation is now on an irreversible historical course.

Following the Party, the Chinese nation has found a path to success. The CPC has grown from an organization with only more than 50 members to the largest Marxist governing party in the world. It has united and led the Chinese people in their billions to make a series of monumental achievements. At a special exhibition for the fight against the Covid-19 pandemic in the Museum of the Communist Party of China, the hanging flags of "Party members teams" show what the key to the victory over Covid-19 in Wuhan was. More than two years ago, under the strong leadership of the CPC Central Committee with Comrade Xi Jinping at its core, China galvanized the entire nation to fight against the pandemic. A total of 346 national medical teams, consisting of more than 40,000 medical workers, rushed to the front lines in Wuhan, Hubei. The majority of them were Party members. I also reported the stories of Wuhan. One page of my interview notebook recorded that February 9, 2020 saw the largest number of incoming medical personnel: a total of 5,787 arrived to defend the city against the virus in 41 flights from 12 provincial-level regions. In Wuhan, I was often moved by every such effort supported by the whole Party and the whole nation. The Chinese people always believe that the CPC is the backbone of them; following the CPC, they will surely prevail over any difficulty or obstacle and the Chinese nation will be able to bring about more miraculous achievements.

Every national Party congress is a milestone for China's development. The First CPC National Congress is described by the Chinese people as an epochal event in China's history. Over one hundred years later, the 20th CPC National Congress has laid out an inspiring blueprint for us to embark on a new journey to build China into a modern socialist country in all respects and advance toward the Second Centenary Goal. It is a groundbreaking event for China.

A song written in 1940 in my hometown in the Yimeng Mountains, a former revolutionary base of the CPC in Shandong Province, has become a classic that is heard around the country. The lyrics are as follows: "You are the lighthouse, shining the sea before daybreak; you are the helmsman, steering the ship. The great Communist Party of China, you are the core, you are the direction." The name of the song is *Following the Communist Party of China*. It expresses the Chinese people's aspiration and clearly shows that history and the people have chosen the Communist Party of China.

Well, that's it from me. Thank you for your attention.

An Interpretation of the 20th CPC National Congress: The Key Role of the CPC

Augusto Soto

Professor of ESADE Business School in Spain,
Director of the "Dialogue with China" Project

At the main entrance of Zhongnanhai in downtown Beijing stands a traditional screen wall inscribed with a slogan in Chinese "为人民服务", meaning "serve the people." This concept is the base to understand the inspiration of China's Communist Party, and how China is governed in contemporary times. Recently this year, in President Xi Jinping's book *The Governance of China IV*, among the various quotes based on Chinese ancient sayings, he brought to the fore one which is particularly important: "The essence of government is livelihood, and the essence of livelihood is sufficiency." In other words, the capacity to deliver. Now, I would like to focus on five points.

First, efficiency, meaning the capacity to deliver. In perspective, the CPC has delivered and in doing so, with a distinctive style. China declared the victory of eliminating absolute poverty within the country in 2021 with nearly 100 million rural poor lifted out of poverty during the last decade. Indeed, as we all know, it has lifted more than 850 million people out of poverty in the last 40 years (the most overwhelming figure in the history of mankind and endorsed by international organizations, including the United Nations).

Second, and related to the previous point: humanistic approach. Furthermore, by the end of last decade several cities and rural areas were clearly closing gaps with advanced countries in life expectancy. In 2019 that indicator showed that in Beijing life expectancy was already 82 years, while in Washington 77, just to quote the most astonishing statistic. But it is still more impressive than that. According to the most recent data in September 2022, China passed the United States in life expectancy. The figure is the outcome of the governance of a country which represents one fifth of the world's population and it should be a headline, not only in the West, but globally.

As a result, third, I stress a wholistic and comprehensive approach. A country like China, an agricultural nation about 70 years ago today boasts the world's most extensive education and social welfare system, the largest high-speed railway network and cutting-edge technologies in many sectors, thanks to its innovative development concepts and forward-looking and viable long-term plans.

The recent 20th CPC National Congress underscored the achievement of China becoming the major trading partner of over 140 countries and regions, leading the globe in the total volume of trade in goods. It accounts for 18.5% of the world economy, up 7.2 percentage points over the past decade.

Fourth: uniqueness. In view of the results accomplished by the Chinese development over the past decades some international analysts may assume that China is advocating its own model or trying to persuade other countries to copy its path.

Xi himself has declared several times that each country has its unique characteristics, and that, above all, it is not wise for a country to try to copy a foreign model without considering its own circumstances. China, thanks to its own history, size and culture (including its political culture) has been following its own path.

The CPC leadership reiterated the point that China's modernization "will not be a replica of the Western one since the Chinese path works well. " Certainly such an evidence is an obvious certainty for several analysts of international affairs worldwide.

Fifth, and last but not least: flexibility. "We must keep to our path and not sway in our commitment. We must not return to the isolation and rigidity of the past, or veer off course by changing our nature or abandoning our system. " Xi said at the recent 20th CPC National Congress. This remark is remarkable, as it is the recognition of the successful path adopted by a country coming from the margins of power and influence several decades ago to the global forefront in the last decade, reflecting perseverance and self-confidence ahead.

Chinese Modernization and Common Prosperity

Sean Slattery

English Expert at the Institute of Party History and Literature
of the CPC Central Committee

Ladies and Gentlemen,

Good afternoon!

The CPC's leadership has been key to China's development over the past decades. It has enabled China to achieve its goal of eliminating absolute poverty, and it will play a crucial rule in the decades to come as China takes concrete steps toward common prosperity. President Xi has identified common prosperity as a defining feature of Chinese modernization. The CPC also considers it a pillar of its people-centered development philosophy, a key aspect of its overall aim of serving the people, and the ultimate goal of development.

Over the last ten years, China has made a lot of headway in promoting common prosperity. My wife's cake shop has given me an insight into this progress. When she opened her store five years ago, the foundations for higher-quality consumption were just taking shape. My wife uses high-quality ingredients for her products, which means charging higher prices. Back then, there was a certain demand for her products, but it was limited to young people with disposable incomes and high-income white-collar workers. At first, growth was slower than expected. But in recent years, her business has expanded, and her customer base covers a broad section of society.

One reason for this growth is the improvement in living standards. As people's incomes have grown, they have gained a greater ability to add extra sweetness to their lives, not just in the form of cakes and desserts but through the consumption of all kinds of products and services of a higher quality. This is reflected in the growth of per capita disposable annual income, which has risen from 16,500 yuan to 35,100 yuan over the past decade.

Growth in personal incomes and an enabling environment have allowed businesses to flourish. Technological innovations and modern logistics have also played an important role, helping companies to reach more customers and lower costs. As these businesses have grown, so have their workforces. My wife started with a team of just three or four and now has a staff of 20. Each of these employees is covered by the state's social security programs, and their earnings are increasing each year.

This is just one part of the story. The changes in rural areas over the past ten years have been more impressive. Thanks to targeted poverty alleviation, China has lifted 98.99 million rural residents, 832 counties, and 128,000 villages from poverty. By making poverty alleviation a top priority, the CPC has fulfilled its pledge not to leave any poverty-stricken area or individual behind in the cause of building a moderately prosperous society.

By improving people's wellbeing, promoting balanced development between regions, eliminating absolute poverty, and realizing moderate prosperity, the CPC has set the stage for China to take concrete steps toward common prosperity in the decades to come.

The CPC has signaled that going forward, it will do more to address regional divides, urban-rural disparities, and the gap in income distribution. These steps are part of a strategy to make the cake bigger and share it out more fairly. This is ultimately about striking the right balance between fairness and efficiency.

Striking this balance has been a perennial challenge for all societies and systems, but only few have been able to get it right. As the governing party, the CPC will have an important role in ensuring China can balance these two factors. And there are several reasons why I think it will be able to effectively fulfill this role.

First, the CPC has accumulated a lot of experience with regard to the challenges involved in promoting efficiency and fairness. This means it is prepared for any potential pitfalls. For example, it has made it clear that common prosperity is not egalitarianism. Efforts will still be focused on encouraging people to realize prosperity through hard work and creativity, while also ensuring the state better plays its role of meeting basic needs and providing services.

Second, it has defined common prosperity as a long-term endeavor. President Xi has stressed that this process must be neither rushed nor delayed. By ensuring gradual and consistent progress toward the goal of common prosperity in the decades to come, China will be able to create plenty of scope for promoting both fairness and efficiency.

Third, the CPC's practice of piloting measures at the local level before rolling them out nationwide will be crucial. A demonstration zone for common prosperity has been set up in Zhejiang. Other localities around the country are also working to develop innovative approaches for promoting common prosperity. I think this kind of local experimentation will provide opportunities for developing innovative solutions, perfecting policies, and addressing potential problems.

Overall, the progress China had made over the past decade has left it well-placed to take significant strides toward common prosperity in the years to come. The future is also looking bright for my wife's business as she is making plans to open a second store.

Thank you!

The Key Role of the Communist Party of China in Various Fields

Sheradil Baktygulov

Director of World Policy Study Institute,

External Expect of National Institute for Strategic Studies of the Kyrgyz Republic

The Communist Party of China has proved to the world that communism is very effective in the modern world. Its 20th National Congress was the most significant event in China this year. China owes much of its achievements over the years to the CPC. The CPC leadership has enabled the Chinese to break free from the shackles of the century of humiliation, develop their economy, become a recognized economic power in the world, and set the model for universal and equitable development.

Because of the CPC's governing achievements, many countries are once again turning their attention to the unique model of governance that China has created, one that takes advantage of a market economy and relies on the support of every citizen. China has eliminated absolute poverty, built a moderately prosperous society in all respects, and is on track to achieve its Second Centenary Goal of becoming a great modern socialist country.

The CPC has always followed its original aspiration. The rejuvenation of the Chinese nation has become an irreversible historical process. Building a moderately prosperous society in all respects is a wonderful goal that the CPC has successfully achieved in the past century. And now the CPC is leading the Chinese people toward the Second Centenary Goal: to build China into a great modern socialist country that is prosperous, strong, democratic, culturally advanced, harmonious, and beautiful by the middle of this century.

Building a moderately prosperous society in all respects is an important commitment of the CPC to the people. The completion of this task means not only raising the country's economic, scientific and technological power to a new level and improving the living standards of all people, but also being able to share Chinese wisdom and Chinese approaches with the international community.

The 20th CPC National Congress proposed to advance the rejuvenation of the Chinese nation on all fronts through a Chinese path to modernization. It is worth noting that Chinese modernization implies the improvement of the living standards of all Chinese people, and that no one will be left behind on the road to common prosperity.

The report to the 20th CPC National Congress states, "We will stand firmly on the right side of history and on the side of human progress. Dedicated to peace, development, cooperation, and mutual benefit, we will strive to safeguard world peace and development as we pursue our own development, and we will make greater contributions to world peace and development through our own development." Indeed, over the past century, the CPC has written a glorious chapter in the history of the development of the Chinese nation and the history of human progress. Generations of Chinese Communists have fought for the independence, strength and wellbeing of their people, and shared their experience with other countries, including in the area of poverty eradication. Chinese President Xi Jinping has repeatedly called at the global level for building a human community with a shared future and an open, inclusive, clean, and beautiful world that enjoys lasting peace, universal security, and common prosperity.

China has proposed the Belt and Road Initiative to strengthen ties between countries through coordinated policies, interconnected infrastructure, free trade and investment financial cooperation, and cultural exchanges. Through this initiative, China provides public goods to the world and advocates the Silk Road Spirit of peace and cooperation, openness and inclusiveness, mutual learning and mutual benefit.

The report to the 20th CPC National Congress states, "As a collaborative endeavor, the Belt and Road Initiative has been welcomed by the international community both as a public good and a cooperation platform. China has become a major trading partner for more than 140 countries and regions, it leads the world in total volume of trade in goods, and it is a major destination for global investment and a leading country in outbound investment. Through these efforts, we have advanced a broader agenda of opening up across more areas and in greater depth." Promoting the Belt and Road Initiative based on the principle of achieving shared growth through discussion and collaboration shows the openness of the CPC.

If we analyze the 100-year history of the CPC, it is easy to see that the CPC has always been open to outside ideas. Not only did the CPC play the greatest role in the long and difficult struggle for national liberation, but it also worked hard to improve the governance of the country after the founding of the People's Republic of China, especially after the reform and opening up policy was adopted in the late 1970s.

Thanks to the willingness of its leaders to learn from developed countries, China has found a development path that is appropriate to its national conditions and has developed into the world's second largest economy in the 30 years since its reform and opening up, raising the living standards of its people and contributing to global economic growth. Since reform and opening up, China has lifted more than 850 million people out of poverty and achieved the goal of eradicating poverty by 2030, as set out in the United Nations Sustainable Development Agenda, a decade ahead of schedule.

The 20th CPC National Congress called on all Chinese people to strive in unity to build a modern socialist country in all respects and advance national rejuvenation on all fronts. I believe that under the leadership of the CPC and guided by its farsighted policies, the Chinese people, with their unlimited potential, will be able to achieve this goal.

Chinese Modernization

To Advance the Rejuvenation of the Chinese Nation on All Fronts Through a Chinese Path to Modernization

Zhao Cheng

Vice President of Xinhua News Agency, Executive Deputy Director of the Academic Committee of New China Research, Xinhua News Agency

The 20th National Congress of the Communist Party of China, which just concluded, drew a grand blueprint for building a modern socialist country in all respects and advancing the great rejuvenation of the Chinese nation on all fronts. General Secretary Xi Jinping profoundly expounded on the scientific connotation, Chinese features, and essential requirements of the Chinese path to modernization and highlighted the importance to advance the rejuvenation of the Chinese nation on all fronts through a Chinese path to modernization.

Here, I would like to share with you some understanding of this topic.

First, China succeeded in advancing and expanding Chinese modernization.

Modernization is the common pursuit of mankind since the industrial civilization and a long-cherished dream since the start of the modern era. Over the past 100 years since the founding of the CPC, all efforts made by the Chinese people under the leadership of the Party are to build China into a modern power and realize the great rejuvenation of the Chinese nation. Based on our decades of exploration and practice since the founding of the People's Republic of China in 1949, especially since the launch of reform and opening up in 1978, as well as the new breakthroughs made in theory and practice since the 18th CPC National

Congress, we have succeeded in advancing and expanding Chinese modernization.

Over the past 10 years, the Party led the Chinese to win the largest battle against poverty in human history, and close to 100 million poor rural residents have been lifted out of poverty, which changed the fate of countless ordinary people in the country.

Recently, we learned about the story of Jihao Youguo, a girl living in the Daliang Mountains in southwest China. Everyone once lived in earthen shelters in this region, with an average altitude of over 2,500 meters known as a "poor corner of China." Before the age of 10, Jihao Youguo had never seen the outside world, and a dilapidated, dark earthen house with low ceilings and leaking roofs was her home. But now, the 14-year-old girl lives with her family in a new apartment of 100 m^2 and attends a junior high school in the city. Over 1 million poverty-stricken people in the Daliang Mountains like Jihao Youguo have gotten rid of poverty and started a promising new life.

The complete victory in eradicating absolute poverty is a big step for China to achieve modernization. The country completed industrialization that took developed countries hundreds of years in just a few decades and created the rare miracles of fast economic growth and long-term social stability. In 2021, China's GDP topped 114 trillion yuan, accounting for 18.5% of the world economy, and its per capita GDP was close to the threshold for high-income economies. The country also has built the largest education, social security, and healthcare systems in the world. Today, China enjoys the world's largest networks of high-speed railways and expressways and witnessed major successes on multiple fronts, including manned spaceflight, lunar and Martian exploration, quantum information, and new energy technology.

The report to the 20th CPC National Congress clarified a two-step strategic plan to build China into a great modern socialist country in all respects: basically realizing socialist modernization from 2020 through 2035; building China into a great modern socialist country that is prosperous, strong, democratic, culturally advanced, harmonious, and beautiful from 2035 through the middle of this century.

Second, we should have a deep understanding of Chinese modernization that is characterized by features that are unique to the Chinese context.

Chinese modernization is socialist modernization pursued under the leadership of the CPC. It contains elements that are common to the modernization processes of all countries, but it is more characterized by features that are unique to the Chinese context. The report to the 20th CPC National Congress lists the five features: the modernization of a huge population; the modernization of common prosperity for all; the modernization of material and cultural-ethical advancement; the modernization of harmony between humanity and nature; and the modernization of peaceful development.

So far, the total population of countries and regions that have achieved modernization worldwide has not exceeded 1 billion. China is working to achieve modernization for more than 1.4 billion people. When the goal is completed, the number of people in the world achieving modernization will be more than doubled, which is expected to completely rewrite the world's landscape of modernization. This is a task of unparalleled difficulty and complexity; it inevitably means that our pathways of development and methods of advancement will be unique.

Chinese culture espouses the principle of promoting harmony between humanity and nature, emphasizing that man and nature are a community of life. In pursuing modernization, China will not tread the old path of developing the economy at the cost of the environment. We will protect nature and the environment as we do our own lives. We will continue to pursue a model of sound development featuring improved production, higher living standards, and healthy ecosystems.

Let me give you an example. The Yangtze finless porpoise has lived on the earth for 25 million years. It is the only mammal in the Yangtze River, known as the "giant panda in the water." However, it was almost extinct. A few days ago, the Ministry of Agriculture and Rural Affairs of the People's Republic of China announced the preliminary results of the field studies on the Yangtze finless porpoises in the whole Yangtze River basin in 2022. In many places of the upper, middle and lower reaches of the Yangtze River, the researchers found large groups of a dozen of the Yangtze finless porpoises, and especially the number of groups of mother and child Yangtze finless porpoises increased significantly. Moreover, the Yangtze finless porpoise has even been found in sections where there used to be no trace of the species. The 10-year fishing ban is being enforced on the Yangtze River, the largest river in China. More than 200,000 fishermen along the Yangtze River have relinquished their nets, promoting the natural regeneration of the mother.

The immutable goal of Chinese modernization drive is to meet the people's aspirations for a better life. We will endeavor to maintain and promote social fairness and justice, and promote all-around material abundance as well as people's well-rounded development. In addition to creating more material and cultural wealth, we need also to provide more quality ecological goods to meet people's ever-growing demands for a beautiful environment.

Third, we must firmly adhere to the essential requirements of Chinese modernization.

The report to the 20th CPC National Congress said that the essential requirements of Chinese modernization are as follows: upholding the leadership of the CPC and socialism with Chinese characteristics, pursuing high-quality development, developing whole-process people's democracy, enriching the people's cultural lives, achieving common prosperity for all, promoting harmony between humanity and nature, building a human community with a shared future, and creating a new form of human advancement.

Only by accurately grasping these essential requirements can we understand how China will advance the rejuvenation of the Chinese nation on all fronts through a Chinese path to modernization.

In terms of the defining feature, Chinese modernization is socialist modernization pursued under the leadership of the CPC. Upholding the leadership of the CPC is the most salient feature and the most outstanding strength of Chinese modernization, and is the overarching principle that must be upheld in following a Chinese path to modernization. Following the path of socialism with Chinese characteristics is the most essential requirement of advancing Chinese modernization.

In terms of the scientific meaning, the goal of advancing Chinese modernization is to build China into a great modern socialist country that is prosperous, strong, democratic, culturally advanced, harmonious, and beautiful. To this end, China must scale new heights in every dimension of material, political, cultural-ethical, social, and ecological advancement. In order to achieve new heights in every dimension of material advancement, we must pursue high-quality development. The report to the 20th CPC National Congress made it clear that to build a modern socialist country in all respects, we must, first and foremost, pursue high-quality development, which further highlights the overall and far-reaching significance of the quality of development.

In terms of international influence, realizing national development and rejuvenation in a peaceful way is a salient feature of Chinese modernization. Chinese modernization has blazed a path to modernization for developing countries, explored a new model of development featuring win-win cooperation, joint contribution and shared benefits, and provided Chinese insight and input to help solve common challenges of humanity.

Let me share the story of a delegate to the 20th CPC National Congress. Lin Zhanxi, a 79-year-old mushroom grass expert at a university in Fujian Province, China, has been devoted his life to research on how to "replace trees with grass" to grow mushrooms to increase farmers' income, control sandstorms, generate power and make paper. For more than 30 years, the grass he has developed has been planted in deserts, the Gobi Desert and the banks of the Yellow River in China, and then been promoted in more than 100 countries and regions. From South Pacific Island Countries to Africa and Latin America, many people have got rid of poverty by using those grass to grow mushrooms. This is the epitome of China's efforts to deliver greater benefits to all peoples with its own development through a Chinese path to modernization.

An ancient civilization with a history of more than 5,000 years is striding towards modernization, which is a wonderful enterprising story and high-profile epic on the blue planet. Under the leadership of the CPC, the Chinese people, full of confidence, are advancing national rejuvenation on all fronts through a Chinese path to modernization. China's new development results will surely update the world on a Chinese path.

Chinese Modernization: Concept and Translation

Zhang Shiyi

Director-General of the Sixth Research Department of the Institute of
Party History and Literature of the CPC Central Committee

"Chinese modernization" is one of the key concepts in the report to the 20th CPC National Congress. This concept has been mentioned by General Secretary Xi Jinping in many occasions, and its Chinese characteristics and essential requirements are articulated specifically and systematically again in the report. For such a concept, the delegates to the Congress conducted in-depth discussions on it and the international media also paid close attention to it.

It is not hard to understand, as we have completed the First Centenary Goal of building a moderately prosperous society in all respects and the task ahead is to work toward the Second Centenary Goal of building China into a great modern socialist country. In other words, to realize modernization has become our immediate goal and practical task.

Indeed, modernization is one of the common goals pursued by all humanity. Though developed countries in the West have achieved modernization, most developing countries, China included, are still working hard to realize this goal. Since the founding of the People's Republic of China and particularly after entering the new era, through constant experiment and practice, our Party has deepened its understanding, become more mature strategically, and accumulated abundant practice in building a modern socialist country. It has successfully advanced and expanded Chinese modernization and created a new model for human advancement. Chinese modernization is deeply rooted in China and is suited to China's conditions, thus boasting great development potential.

The reason why China could pioneer a new path of modernization is that we have unique cultural traditions, history, and national conditions, which dictates that we must adopt a path of development that is consistent with our own unique characteristics.

We can also see this from the following two aspects. First, China is a major country with unique characteristics, so it must independently decide its own future and take its own path without following suit or sitting on the fence. We must develop our country and our nation with our own strength, and we must maintain a firm grasp on the future of China's development and progress. Second, during the historical process of achieving modernization, China, as a late comer, could not only learn from the useful experiences of developed countries in realizing this goal, but also avoid their twists and turns and mistakes. In this way, China could go faster, better, and more stable on the path toward Chinese modernization, and thus create miracles of rapid economic growth and enduring social stability. It is fair to say that the advancement and expansion of Chinese modernization show the superiority of socialism with Chinese characteristics and dispel the myth that "modernization is westernization," offering new options for other developing countries to achieve modernization.

How should we look at the statements on "Chinese modernization" in the report? I think the key is to understand and grasp its nature and positioning.

It is pointed out in the report that Chinese modernization is socialist modernization pursued under the leadership of the Communist Party of China. This clearly explains the nature of Chinese modernization which is different from capitalist modernization centered on capital in western countries, it is people-centered socialist modernization. Based on traditional Chinese culture, it is capable of overcoming great disparity in wealth, materialism, consumerism, and other shortcomings in capitalist society due to pursuing maximum profits by capital. It advocates "people's well-rounded development" rather than development of "one-dimensional man" under the capitalist system.

The report also clarifies the five characteristics of Chinese modernization and articulates its essential requirements in nine sentences. These statements help us understand the positioning of Chinese modernization: a great, independent, integral, and advanced concept as opposed to western modernization. Based on such understandings, we translate the concept into "Chinese modernization" in the English version. This translation is concise and straightforward and is applicable in translating the concept into other foreign languages. This helps spread the concept in the international context. Seen from the reports and feedbacks from mainstream foreign media during the 20th CPC National Congress, this English translation is commonly recognized and used and spreads quickly in the international community, achieving the expected communication effect.

National Rejuvenation and People's Wellbeing: Two Keys to Understanding Chinese Modernization

Yang Mingwei

Director-General of the International Department of the Institute of
Party History and Literature of the CPC Central Committee

While talking about the outlook of Chinese Communists on development and modernization, General Secretary Xi Jinping said that "Working for the wellbeing of the people and the rejuvenation of the nation is the immutable aim of our Party in leading the modernization drive, and the root and soul of the new development philosophy. We will only have the right view of development and modernization if we follow a people-centered approach, insisting that development is for the people, reliant on the people, and that its fruits should be shared by the people." He also emphasized that it is what we have upheld that has enabled us to successfully advance and expand Chinese modernization through long-term exploration and practice.

It shows that Chinese modernization is closely linked with people's wellbeing and national rejuvenation.

1. Chinese modernization is closely linked with the great rejuvenation of the Chinese nation

Chinese modernization is inseparable from national rejuvenation. It has been developed as we pursue national rejuvenation. All the endeavors through which the

Party has united and led the Chinese people since its founding have been tied together by one ultimate theme—developing China into a great modern socialist country and bringing about the great rejuvenation of the Chinese nation. Promoting national rejuvenation through the path of Chinese modernization is also the mission and task of Chinese Communists in the new era.

  The Party's understanding of Chinese modernization has gradually deepened along with its explorations of realizing national rejuvenation. After it came to power, the Party has been advancing toward the goals of building a modern socialist country and realizing national rejuvenation. To this end, the Party has led the whole country in promoting economic and social development by implementing five-year plans one after another and setting long-range objectives, so as to gradually move toward the goal of a modern socialist country. Though our understanding of the connotation of modernization was not comprehensive enough at first, we have never wavered on our goal toward modernization and never stopped deepening our understanding. As early as in 1964, the Party had proposed a two-step strategy while formulating the Third Five-Year Plan. The first step was to establish an independent and relatively complete industrial system and economic system within 15 years starting from the Third Five-Year Plan period, and the second step was to realize the modernization of industry, agriculture, national defense, and science and technology in another 15 years by the end of the 20th century. When our country entered a new period marked by the launch of reform and opening up, the Party set the grand objective of building a prosperous, powerful, democratic, and culturally advanced socialist country. After Chinese socialism entered a new era, the Party proposed at its 19th National Congress a new two-step strategy from an even higher starting point. In the first stage of 15 years from 2020 to 2035, China will, on the basis of moderate prosperity in full, strive to basically realize socialist modernization. In the second stage of another 15 years from 2035 to the middle of the 21st century, building on basically achieved modernization, China will strive to turn itself into a great modern socialist country that is prosperous, strong, democratic, culturally advanced, harmonious, and beautiful. The 20th CPC National Congress reaffirmed the two-step strategy for building a great modern socialist country in all respects.

After considering the logic relation between Chinese modernization and national rejuvenation, we can easily come to the conclusion that the Party has constantly deepened its understanding of and improved its strategy for building a modern socialist country, and gradually enriched its practice in this regard. The Party and the people have never wavered in their will and determination to build a modern socialist country. History has proved and will continue to prove that the historical course of Chinese modernization is irreversible, as is the historical trend of promoting national rejuvenation through the path of Chinese modernization.

2. One important objective for Chinese modernization is to achieve common prosperity

Common prosperity is a key indicator of the people's wellbeing. Achieving common prosperity for all is both a persistent goal for our Party and an essential requirement of Chinese modernization. Chinese Communists' pursuit of for "common prosperity" has a long history.

Achieving common prosperity is a basic question that Marxist theory needs to resolve and what Marx and Engels envisaged in socialist society and communist society. Since its founding, the Communist Party of China has consciously shouldered the historic responsibility of resolving this question and making this vision a reality. After the founding of the People's Republic of China in 1949, Chairman Mao Zedong pointed out that under the leadership of the CPC, China "can grow more prosperous and in strength year by year, and we will see that happen. The prosperity is shared prosperity and the strength is also shared by all the people." In the early 1980s, against the backdrop of reform and opening up,

Comrade Deng Xiaoping constantly reminded us, "We keep to the socialist road in order to attain the ultimate goal of common prosperity." As Chinese socialism entered a new era, the Party Central Committee with Comrade Xi Jinping at its core has given high priority to "achieving solid progress in promoting common prosperity" and stressed that "bringing about common prosperity is a defining feature of socialism with Chinese characteristics and an important mission of the Communist Party of China," that "it is crucial to focus due attention on the issue of common prosperity," and that "we must move steadily toward the goal of common prosperity for all."

As China secured a complete victory in its fight against poverty and a moderately prosperous society in all respects in 2020, a substantial step forward has been made in the CPC's efforts to unite and lead the people in the pursuit for better lives and common prosperity. China has made historic achievements in solving the problem of absolute poverty that has plagued the Chinese nation for thousands of years, and brought about a miracle in humanity's history of poverty reduction. This has laid a solid foundation for building a modern socialist country in all respects and created favorable conditions for realizing the Second Centenary Goal.

It can be said with certainty that only under the firm leadership of the CPC could we mobilize the whole Party and the entire nation to lift the people out of poverty, and only Chinese Communists can take on such a great historic task, lead the people in moving on toward the goal of common prosperity, and eventually resolve this major question.

Chinese Modernization Includes the Idea of a More Equitable and Fairer Society

Martin Jacques

Renowned British scholar, Expert in China affairs

One of the most interesting questions to arise at the 20th CPC National Congress concerned Chinese modernization.

Now modernization, the theme of modernization, the problem of modernization, takes us right back to China and the early 19th century, when it failed to industrialize at the same time or soon after Britain and other European countries.

In fact, it was 150 years later from 1949 that China really embarked on a strategy of modernization.

And this largely informed the Communist Party's efforts after 1949, especially after 1978, when the strategy of modernization under Deng Xiaoping and subsequent leaders dominated China's attempts to enter the world on economically prosperous and also strong basis.

Now that modernization in this whole period really was inevitably in the shadow of the west.

And therefore, China was always in some degree or other overwhelmingly forced to learn from the western model, to, in some ways, imitate the western model, because that was really the best course of action.

That never meant that it was simply westernized the western modernization, because China had to adapt the western model to its own circumstances.

So it was always very distinctive, actually, even during this period.

But nonetheless, I think it's a broad generalization. We can say, modernization hitherto has been largely based on the western style template.

Now, the Congress raises a really interesting question, which is, we've now got to a period where... we're not at the American level yet, but in some areas, we are. Technologically, we become very innovative. The economy is now the second largest in the world, by some measures, the largest economy in the world.

And so we've got you a point now where we need to think very afresh about the nature of modernization.

What is appropriate for China in terms of modernization? What is appropriate for a socialist country in terms of modernization?

Here, I think the question being posed is an absolutely fascinating one, because it opens up huge new possibilities for China's development in the future.

But I don't want to go into all that now. I just want to take one example. And that is common prosperity.

Now, common prosperity is really, I think, a response in many ways to a period of Chinese development, which, above all, emphasized economic growth, and which, led to very high levels of inequality.

I mean China's Gini coefficient is probably on a par with, if not higher than that of the United States.

Now, obviously, for a socialist country, this is, in the long run, unacceptable.

It needs to be significantly reduced. A different kind of society needs to be built, a society that is inclusive rather than exclusive, that believes the fairness and equity lies at the heart of a progressive society.

So I think what China's embrace of Chinese modernization will centrally include is the idea of a more equitable and fairer society.

Now, the implications of this for China's position in the world are very interesting, because basically joined the whole era of American style globalization, this led to inequality left, right and center across the world led by the United States.

And China was also, to some extent, drawn into that because of the type of modernization that existed in the world at that time.

Now, what happens when China adopts a different kind of modernization, which at the heart of it is fairness and equity.

And it seems to me that if China can be successful at this in the way that it's been so successful at eliminating extreme poverty, then the impact of this, China's impact on the world in introducing the central theme of development, fairness and equity, will be enormous.

The Chinese Modernization Offers New Options and Opportunities to the World

Peggy Cantave Fuyet

French Expert at the Institute of Party History and Literature of the CPC Central Committee

The Chinese modernization is a term that is stressed in the report to the 20th National Congress of the Communist Party of China. It is said to be a modernization which, on the one side, contains elements that are common to the modernization of all countries, but on the other, has features that are unique to the Chinese context.

Today, I would like to share with you my understanding of the Chinese path to modernization which, I believe, can inspire other countries and offer new options and opportunities to the world.

1. China's practice shows that there can be different paths to modernization

When China entered the World Trade Organization in 2001, some people, especially in the West, thought that China was going to and could only follow the Western model of modernization. This is a misunderstanding of China. China has never wanted to copy the Western model of modernization, neither it wanted to impose its model on other countries. China wants to follow its own path to achieve modernization, a socialist modernization that is people-centered, attaches great importance to protecting the environment and promotes peaceful development.

Moreover, China is willing to share its experiences and benefits with the world.

2. The modernization path of Western countries has major flaws

The Western modernization has provided material wealth mainly for a minority of the world population in the Western developed countries, based on the exploitation of the great majority, on imperialism, colonialism and hegemony. It has caused more social injustice, exploitation, wars, territorial expansions, oppression of other populations, waste of natural resources, pollution, unbalanced and unsustainable development, and so on. This is not the path China wants to follow.

3. The Chinese modernization is different from the Western model and suits China's national conditions

The Chinese modernization is a modernization that suits China's national conditions, follows the path of socialism with Chinese characteristics, relies on the people and is for the people's benefit. It promotes a development that brings common prosperity not only to the 1% or 10%, and not even only to the majority of the Chinese people, but to each single one of them.

The Chinese modernization is also reversing the trend of developing at the expense of the environment and promotes a balanced, qualitative and sustainable development which allows a harmonious coexistence between humans and nature. Production, well-being of the population and preservation of the environment are considered as an inseparable whole in the process of development.

The Chinese modernization is, moreover, not following the path of imperialism, of colonialism, or of hegemony, but the path of peaceful development. Indeed, China's development is based on cooperation, equality, mutual respect, and mutual benefits. The Belt and Road Initiative is a concrete example of this, and although this initiative was launched by China, it is about developing in common and sharing together with all countries the fruits of development.

Finally, the Chinese modernization uses the Chinese wisdom and approach to propose solutions to solve common problems faced by humankind. The Marxist perspective and method and some progressive Chinese traditional concepts are used to analyze the world and address problems faced by China and the other countries today, embracing, for instance, the Chinese traditional concept that "all under heaven we are one family" and the Marxist concept that "the free development of each is the condition for the free development of all."

4. The impact of the Chinese modernization on the world

The Chinese modernization has and will have more and more impact on the world, not only because it contributes to the development of other countries, especially the developing countries which were plundered and left behind in the process of Western modernization, but also because it shows other countries that it is possible to follow a path of modernization different from the Western model and that this new path can provide other countries a win-win way of achieving their own modernization; they can choose from the Chinese modernization experience, the elements that are suitable for them according to their own conditions and needs, and continue to develop while keeping their independence and autonomy.

Therefore, while pursuing its own modernization, China offers a new path to modernization that can serve as a source of inspiration for other countries, and makes a greater contribution in promoting human progress, world peace and development, as well as building an ecological civilization and a human community with a shared future.

China's Modernization and Global Cooperation

Khalid Taimur Akram

Executive Director, Pakistan Research Center for a Community with Shared Future (PRCCSF) & CEO, RK Consultants, Islamabad

My name is Khalid Taimur Akram, and I am the Executive Director for Pakistan Research Center for a Community with Shared Future (PRCCSF) & CEO, RK Consultants, Islamabad. I would like to express my gratitude to the organizers of this grand conference, and thank you very much for inviting me. It is indeed a great platform that we all have gathered to understand the outcomes of the 20th National Congress of CPC. I would like to talk about Chinese modernization in this era and future prospects for cooperation.

Countries around the world faced challenges in their journey towards modernization. However, China has been progressing towards that goal under the visionary leadership of His Excellency, President Xi Jinping. China has adopted modernization in last 10 years in a very, very rapid pace. Modernization can be defined as the transformation of a traditional or less developed society into a modern and industrialized society. China's rapid economic development reflects this shift.

In the first stage, China's journey towards modernization, the leadership's goal was to end the old established system and to establish People's Republic. The second stage saw the leadership exploring new governance mechanism and focus on economic recovery through industrialization. In the third stage, since the larger launching of the reform and opening up, the leadership's main goal has been to create a pragmatic development concept and take into account national agenda.

For the past couple of years, its goal has been to turn China into a modern country and realize the Chinese dream. I believe that reform and opening up and robust planning have enabled China to transform itself from a highly centralized planned economy into a full market economy with a variety of industries in it, and largely closed country, which people used to think, is now one of the most vibrant economies and open economies of the world. China has also taken historically from a country constrained by backward productive forces. It has become the world's second largest economy and raised people's living standard from low level to the moderate prosperity level. These achievements have created robust institutional conditions and late material base for rapid development, taking the country towards modernization and at national level.

Dear all, the world is undergoing profound changes, economic development and modernization have not only boosted global growth, but also deepened the broadened and global cooperation. Yet modernization and globalization have also created many challenges, especially for some developing countries, which need to be addressed. In this aspect, there are lessons other countries can learn from China's development governance system, and modernization model, and use them to meet their respective challenges on road to modernization. Socialism with Chinese characteristics which China follows defines the leadership's approach to governing the country. An essence of socialism with Chinese characteristics is to develop the productive forces.

I believe that China's soft power has also played a role in its modernization drive. The country has built up enormous assets in terms of soft power, which have contributed its rise to the global stage. It is true that great visions are simple and pure, but they require actions to be turned into reality. No matter how practical and sound a plan is, it cannot succeed without proper implementation. Thereby, the modernization of China represents deep gradual changes into the country's economy, politics and society. These changes do not mean rejection of the existing values and norms. Instead, it means reforming the existing society.

And the last, I would also like to comment on the 20th National Congress of the Communist Party of China that has been held very successfully. China has been blessed once again with President Xi Jinping's leadership who is the most dynamic and popular leader in the world. I believe that under his guidance and robust policies, the country will enhance its global outreach, will work on the plans made for the next five years, and will create enthusiasm and victory.

Thank you very much.

China's Fine Traditional Culture

On China's Fine Traditional Culture

Wang Junwei

Chairman of the Academic and Editorial Council of the Institute of Party History and Literature of the CPC Central Committee (vice minister level), Executive Vice Chairman of the National High-Level Think Tank Council of the Institute of Party History and Literature of the CPC Central Committee

Distinguished Guests,

Ladies and Gentlemen,

Good afternoon.

In his report to the 20th National Congress of the Communist Party of China, General Secretary Xi Jinping noted, "Chinese Communists are keenly aware that only by integrating the basic tenets of Marxism with China's specific realities and fine traditional culture and only by applying dialectical and historical materialism can we provide correct answers to the major questions presented by the times and discovered through practice and can we ensure that Marxism always retains its vigor and vitality."

It is difficult to give a detailed explanation in the limited time on the long history of China's fine traditional culture and the rich ideas it contains, so my focus will be on three points.

1. China's fine traditional culture provides an unfailing source of aspirations for the Chinese nation

In a long history of well over 5,000 years, the Chinese people have developed a unique, extensive, and profound culture. This fine traditional culture runs in the blood of the Chinese people and has become a part of the genes of the Chinese nation. Why do I say this traditional culture gives us an unfailing support? Because we Chinese people today still preserve, respect, and apply it. Confucius is a figure of over 2,500 years ago, but we today still read, study, and live by his words. I'm very happy to see that today's forum is attended by friends from all over the world. This is what Confucius said, "What a joy it is to have friends coming from afar!" China will not allow itself to be bullied by hegemonism, nor will it bully countries that are small or weak. This is what Confucius meant when he said, "Do not to others what you would not have others do to you."

Chinese culture is exceptionally resilient and appealing. In China's history, herdsmen groups in the north conquered the inland several times, but they all, without exception, then succumbed to Chinese culture and soon became a part of the big family of the Chinese nation, and in this process further developed Chinese culture. This is why we say there is no such logic in traditional Chinese culture that a powerful country is destined for hegemony; China will never become a country seeking hegemony.

China's fine traditional culture espouses many important principles and concepts, such as pursuing common good for all; regarding the people as the foundation of the state; governing by virtue; discarding the outdated in favor of the new; selecting officials on the basis of merit; promoting harmony between humanity and nature; ceaselessly pursuing self-improvement; embracing the world with virtue; acting in good faith and being friendly to others; and fostering neighborliness. These maxims, which have taken shape over centuries of work and life, reflect the Chinese people's way of viewing the universe, the world, society, and morality and are an invaluable source of intellectual wealth and support for the Chinese nation.

2. The CPC has kept China's fine traditional culture alive and strong

More than 80 years ago when the CPC was still weak, Mao Zedong said, "From Confucius to Sun Yat-sen, we should take stock of our history and carry on this valuable legacy." General Secretary Xi Jinping also stressed, "We must not discard the fine cultural traditions of the Chinese nation; on the contrary, we must carry them on because they are the base and the soul of the Chinese nation, and without them, we will lose our roots." Several days ago, General Secretary Xi Jinping paid an inspection visit to the Yinxu archaeological site in Anyang, Henan Province. The oracle-bone inscriptions excavated there shows us the characters used by Chinese 3,000 years ago. From then on, China's cultural traditions have continued unbroken to this day, which is something not seen in any other country in the world. In its century-long history, the CPC has always worked to keep China's fine traditional culture alive and strong.

I will give a few examples here. The goal of we Chinese Communists is to realize Communism, which is highly consistent with a *Datong* society, or a society of universal harmony, which was cherished by ancient Chinese philosophers. Both they and we wish to build an ideal society with no oppression, exploitation, or deception. The CPC's fundamental purpose is to serve the people wholeheartedly, which is a manifestation of the conception "the people create history" of Marxist historical materialism as well as a continuation of the ideas espoused in China's cultural traditions which regard the people as the foundation of the state and rank the people as the highest. The Party's line of thinking is to seek truth from facts, which are words dating from the Han Dynasty and draw on the best of China's traditional culture.

In the noble minds of Chinese Communists, there are many elements from the cultural gems of the Chinese nation passed on over thousands of years, which are in essence an endogenous continuation of fine traditional Chinese culture. For instance, where does the spirit of ceaselessly pursuing self-improvement originate? It was noted 3,000 years ago in the *Book of Changes*, which reads "Just as heaven maintains vigor through movement, greatness demands that one unceasingly pursue self-improvement." The spirit of fearing no sacrifice was recorded 2,300 years ago in *Lü's Commentaries of History*, which reads "Each and every one of us in the army would face death without fear." The goal of the CPC's foreign policy is to safeguard world peace and promote common development, and General Secretary Xi Jinping has proposed the idea of building a human community with a shared future, to build "an open, inclusive, clean, and beautiful world that enjoys lasting peace, universal security, and common prosperity." The word "peace" is a very important concept in China's cultural traditions.

This oracle Chinese character "龢" means peace. It is composed of two parts: on the left, 龠(yue) is a kind of bamboo musical instrument; on the right, 禾(he) means crops or grains. So combining these two parts together, peace comes with music and food.

We hope, by following the principle of shared growth through discussion and collaboration, to safeguard world peace and build a human community with a shared future. This idea of our Chinese Communists represents a continuation and enhancement of China's traditional culture.

Marxism is the theoretical bedrock for Chinese Communists. When upholding and developing Marxism, the CPC has integrated the basic tenets of Marxism with China's specific realities and fine traditional culture. Chinese Communists firmly believe that only by integrating the essence of Marxism with the best of fine traditional Chinese culture and with the common values that our people intuitively apply in their everyday lives can we keep endowing Marxist theory with distinctive Chinese features and consolidating the historical basis and public support for adapting Marxism to the Chinese context and the needs of our times and can we ensure that Marxism puts down deep roots in China.

For more than one hundred years, Chinese Communists have set off contemporary energy of Chinese culture, elevated contemporary relevance of values in Chinese philosophy, and increased the global significance of Chinese wisdom. So we can say with great pride that Chinese Communists have been truly upholding fundamental principles while breaking new ground for fine traditional Chinese culture.

3. China is committed to learning from each other, drawing on each other's strengths, and achieving common progress with all other cultures in the world

We are committed to carrying on China's fine traditional culture, but we never say that China's traditional culture is superior. Over 3,000 years ago, our ancient philosophers had enlightened us, "The more you learn, the less you feel you know" and "One loses by pride and gains by modesty." It is a tradition in Chinese culture to accept all good advice and progress with the times. Stubbornly adhering to one's tradition and rejecting any foreign culture would only result in one's own culture suffering "anemia," withering, or even dying out. Every nation and culture in the world has its own strength that China can learn from.

In recent years, many Chinese young people like wearing *Hanfu*. *Hanfu* is the traditional Chinese clothing and is an important part of China's cultural traditions, but we will not reject lounge suit just because we like *Hanfu*, and most of us in attendance today are wearing lounge suits. Different cultures and traditions do not have to be in conflict; they can rather coexist and develop together. Just as sunlight is composed of seven colors, so too our world is full of color and splendor. Every country or nation has its own historical and cultural traditions and its own strengths, and what we should do is to respect each other, learn from each other, draw on each other's strengths, and achieve common progress.

Thank you!

Vigorously Promoting Fine Traditional Chinese Culture and Continuously Adapting Marxism to the Chinese Context and the Needs of Our Times

Liu Ronggang

Director-General of the Seventh Research Department of the Institute of Party History and Literature of the CPC Central Committee

In the report to the 20th National Congress of the Communist Party of China, it is stated, "With a history stretching back to antiquity, China's fine traditional culture is extensive and profound; it is the crystallization of the wisdom of Chinese civilization. Our traditional culture espouses many important principles and concepts, including pursuing common good for all; regarding the people as the foundation of the state; governing by virtue; discarding the outdated in favor of the new; selecting officials on the basis of merit; promoting harmony between humanity and nature; ceaselessly pursuing self-improvement; embracing the world with virtue; acting in good faith and being friendly to others; and fostering neighborliness. These maxims, which have taken shape over centuries of work and life, reflect the Chinese people's way of viewing the universe, the world, society, and morality and are highly consistent with the values and propositions of scientific socialism." The report not only clarifies the path and direction for adapting Marxism to the Chinese context and the needs of our times, but also is of great significance for correctly understanding the status and better exerting the role of China's fine traditional culture.

The traditional Chinese culture developed under the triple influence of Confucianism, Buddhism, and Taoism. The formation and evolution of its essential thoughts and values underwent several historical periods, including the contention of "hundred schools of thought" dating back to the Spring and Autumn and Warring States periods, the prosperity of Confucian classics in the Han Dynasty, the popularity of metaphysics during the period of the Wei, Jin, Southern and Northern Dynasties, the coexistence of Confucianism, Buddhism, and Taoism in the Sui and Tang Dynasties, and the development of the Confucian school of idealist philosophy in the Song and Ming Dynasties.

The traditional Chinese culture embodies a wealth of philosophical ideas, humanistic concepts, edifying values, and moral principles. These include the ideal of great harmony believing that "when the path is just, the common good will reign over all under Heaven"; the tradition of pursuing great unity with all regions following similar customs and all people belonging to one family; the people-centered philosophy holding that the people have primacy over the ruler and the aim of governance is to ensure and improve the people's wellbeing; the idea of ensuring equality among all people in terms of social status and wealth and helping the poor with the wealth of the rich; the pursuit of justice and impartiality of the law; moral standards advocating filial piety, fraternity, loyalty to the country, good faith, propriety, righteousness, integrity, and a sense of shame; the reformist spirit as the old saying goes, "although Zhou was an ancient State, its mission was to make changes"; and the principle of promoting good neighborliness and advocating peace among all countries.

China's fine traditional culture is the cultural origin and lifeline of the Chinese nation. It has not only nourished the enduring growth of the Chinese nation, but also provided important inspiration for resolving challenges confronting humanity today.

Since the 1840s, the Chinese people had been searching assiduously for ways to save the country and the people. During the process, progressives in China, who took the fate of the country as their own responsibility, made a solemn choice to uphold and disseminate Marxist truth. Their choice added vigor to China's fine traditional culture, which in turn provided cultural nourishment for adapting Marxism to the Chinese context and the needs of the times. One reason why Marxism is widely believed in China is because it shares common ground with fine traditional Chinese culture. In 1926, Guo Moruo published an article "Marx Enters a Confucian Temple." In virtue of a fictitious conversation between Marx and Confucius, the article unveils the fact that Marx's pursuit of an ideal society coincides with Confucius's advocating for a world of harmony, demonstrating the similarities between Marxism and Confucianism in some respects. To a certain extent, it also explains why Marxism has been widely spread in China and become the source of inner strength of Chinese communists.

The Communist Party of China has faithfully carried forward the best of China's traditional culture while actively advocating and developing China's advanced culture. During its endeavors over the past century, the CPC has kept deepening understanding of traditional Chinese culture, and its attitude toward traditional culture has gone through changes from "fierce criticism" upon its founding to "inheritance on a critical basis" during the new-democratic revolution period, from "transforming and utilizing" in the period of socialist revolution and construction to "carrying forward" over the period marked by reform, opening up, and socialist modernization, and then to the latest "creative transformation and development" in the new era of socialism with Chinese characteristics.

While adapting the basic tenets of Marxism to China's specific realities, the Party has explored, preserved, and promoted the essence of China's fine traditional culture by following principles such as retaining the essence and rejecting the dross, letting a hundred flowers bloom and a hundred schools of thought contend, and making the past serve the present and bringing forth the new from the old.

These efforts have played an importance role in building up people's inner strength for realizing national rejuvenation, drawing on beneficial philosophies and thinking on national governance, satisfying people's ever growing non-material and cultural demands, and fostering a new generation capable of shouldering the mission of national rejuvenation. In particular, Chinese communists with Comrade Xi Jinping as their chief representative have brought up and championed the shared human values of peace, development, fairness, justice, democracy, and freedom by drawing thoughts and ideas from fine traditional Chinese culture, thus making great contributions to building a human community with a shared future.

General Secretary Xi Jinping pointed out, "At the fundamental level, we owe the success of our Party and socialism with Chinese characteristics to the fact that Marxism works, particularly when it is adapted to the Chinese context and the needs of our times."

To uphold and develop Marxism, and especially to adapt Marxism to the Chinese context and the needs of the times, we must integrate the basic tenets of Marxism with China's specific realities and fine traditional Chinese culture, promote creative transformation and innovative development of fine traditional Chinese culture, and combine the essence of Marxism with the best of fine traditional Chinese culture and with the common values that our people intuitively apply in their everyday lives, thereby helping the most basic cultural genes of the Chinese nation to fit into the socialist system and the call of our era and to connect with contemporary life and the Marxism of contemporary China. Moreover, we must delve into and expound on the contemporary relevance of values in China's fine traditional culture such as benevolence, integrity, righteousness, harmony, unity in diversity, and the people-centered orientation, so as to continue adding new luster to Chinese culture and opening new chapters in adapting Marxism to the Chinese context and the needs of the times.

Carrying Forward Fine Traditional Chinese Culture and Fostering a Strong Sense of Community for the Chinese Nation

Fu Yan

Researcher at Xinhua Institute

During his visit to the Yinxu archaeological site in Anyang, Henan Province on October 28, 2022, General Secretary Xi Jinping said, "Chinese civilization has a long history without discontinuity and has shaped our great nation." China's fine traditional culture is the crystallization of the wisdom of Chinese civilization, and represents the very root and soul of the Chinese nation. Not long ago, Xinhua Institute completed the research on the topic of "fostering a strong sense of community for the Chinese nation." It is also the main task in the work of the Communist Party of China related to ethnic affairs in the new era, and is an important new theory that integrates the basic tenets of Marxism with China's specific realities and fine traditional culture. Based on the study of the 20th CPC National Congress, I'd like to present my understanding about the significance of fine traditional Chinese culture to fostering a strong sense of community for the Chinese nation.

1. Fine traditional Chinese culture is the cultural gene of the core concept of "community for the Chinese nation"

Chinese (zhonghua), an ancient term and concept, is a common name for

China, a country with a long history. In China, all ethnic groups worked together to develop its vast territories, create its long history, and foster a splendid culture and a great national spirit. In history, all ethnic groups' identification with the Chinese political-cultural community centered on the dynasties in the inland, is not only reflected in their recognition for the ruling monarch or the dynasty they lived in, but also in their identification with historical and cultural continuity beyond dynasties.

In 1902, Liang Qichao first put forward the term "the Chinese nation." In an article titled "The Chinese Revolution and the Communist Party of China" published in 1939, Mao Zedong made it clear that "China is a unified country of many ethnic groups and a great nation." The assertion identifies both the existence of different ethnic groups and the concept of the Chinese nation as a whole. Therefore, the concept of "the Chinese nation" entails the concepts of "nationality" and "ethnic group" in Western ethnic theory. It embodies the integration of the Chinese nation as well as the diversity of 56 ethnic groups in China.

"Community for the Chinese nation" is a more specific expression of "the Chinese nation," and an extension with contemporary significance. General Secretary Xi Jinping noted, "Fostering a strong sense of community for the Chinese nation is to guide the Chinese people of all ethnic groups in forging a strong sense of community with a shared future where we rise and fall together." This is a sound and historical summary of the fact that all ethnic groups in the family of the Chinese nation live together, strive together, and pursue common development. The concept of "community for the Chinese nation" contains the profound legacy and cultural gene of fine traditional Chinese culture.

2. Fine traditional Chinese culture is the cultural support for fostering a strong sense of community for the Chinese nation

In the past thousands of years, the Chinese people of all ethnic groups have learned from and integrated with each other, and together created splendid civilization. As the crystallization of the wisdom of Chinese civilization, China's fine traditional culture has become the cultural support for building a shared spiritual home and fostering a strong sense of community for the Chinese nation.

A wealth of ideas on national system and governance espoused in fine traditional Chinese culture are important intellectual and cultural basis for the identification with a unified country of ethnic groups by members in the family of the Chinese nation since ancient times. These ideas have promoted national unity and stability in the long course of history and are also of contemporary value. A major one of them is unification. Since the Qin Dynasty more than 2,000 years ago, unification has always been the overarching political concept of the Chinese nation. All the dynasties either established by the Han people or ethnic minorities took the great unity as their commitment, and regarded their own dynasty as the orthodoxy of a unified multi-ethnic country. This idea played an important role in the formation of the pluralistic integration of the Chinese nation. It can be said that the concept of great unity was a sense of community for the Chinese nation in ancient times.

China's fine traditional culture serves as the cultural foundation of the Chinese nation, and fostering a strong sense of community for the Chinese nation depends on the strong support and continuous empowerment of fine traditional Chinese culture. As an old Chinese saying goes, "Only when the roots are firm and deep can the branches flourish." Only by carrying forward and promoting fine traditional Chinese culture can the community for the Chinese nation be impregnable and the ethnic solidarity and progress be sustainable.

3. Creative transformation and development of fine traditional Chinese culture build up cultural confidence for fostering a strong sense of community for the Chinese nation

The Chinese people's way of viewing the universe, the world, society, and morality in fine traditional Chinese culture is insightful and sage and features an eternal charm across time and space. We must integrate the specific content of fine traditional Chinese culture with the contemporary spirit and modern society, so that all Chinese people build up cultural confidence and strength and come together as a mighty force for realizing national rejuvenation.

Chinese culture integrates the culture of all ethnic groups, and ethnic cultures are an integral part of Chinese culture. General Secretary Xi Jinping has attached great importance to the innovative development of the traditional cultures of ethnic minorities. He pointed out that it is necessary to carry forward and protect the traditional cultures of all ethnic groups, make the past serve the present, develop the new from the old, and strive for creative transformation and innovative development. In the past decade of the new era, China has launched programs to develop literature and film and protect ancient classics of ethnic minorities, ushering in a golden period for the cultural promotion, literary and artistic creation, and industry development of ethnic minorities. Under the great attention and protection of the state, the traditional cultures of ethnic minorities are thriving across the country and adding new luster to Chinese culture.

For example, Gesar is an encyclopedic epic that covers the knowledge system of traditional culture, society, economy, morality and customs of Tibetan, Mongolian, and other ethnic minorities in China. Over the past decades, the Chinese government has spent heavily to preserve and protect the epic. In 2022, the Gesar's story was adapted into an animated film *King Gesar: Trials and Tribulations*, which showcases the epic in a novel way.

Creative transformation and innovative development of fine traditional Chinese culture have consolidated the common intellectual foundation for the whole Party and all Chinese people to strive together in unity, built up cultural confidence for fostering a strong sense of community for the Chinese nation, and inspired the Chinese people of all ethnic groups to stride towards a great modern socialist country.

Traditional Chinese Culture Highlighted in the Report to the 20th National Congress of the Communist Party of China

K. Angelina

Russian Expert at the Institute of Party History and
Literature of the CPC Central Committee

The 20th National Congress of the Communist Party of China, which was recently concluded, is an event of major political importance for the Chinese people and an event that draws the world's attention. I felt truly honored to participate in the translation of the report to the Congress. These days I saw many Russian people discussed about the 20th CPC National Congress on the internet; they talked about Chinese modernization, green and low-carbon development, scientific and technological innovation, and China's cultural confidence and strength.

During the translation process, I was impressed by many expressions about traditional Chinese culture. For example, it was mentioned in the report that to open up a new frontier in adapting Marxism to the Chinese context and the needs of the times, it is imperative to integrate Marxism with China's specific realities. Only by advancing with the times, basing everything on actual conditions, and focusing on solving real problems arising in reform, opening up, and socialist modernization endeavors in the new era, can the Chinese communists find the right answers suited to the realities of China and the needs of our day. It is also imperative to integrate Marxism with China's fine traditional culture. Marxism is the guiding ideology for the CPC and China and China's fine traditional culture is the lifeblood of the Chinese nation. Chinese culture is extensive and profound; it is the crystallization of the wisdom of the Chinese people created over 5,000 years.

China's fine traditional culture is reflected in the country's policies. For example, the concept of pursuing common good for all and regarding the people as the foundation of the state is consistent with the Party's commitment to serving the public good and exercising governance for the people. The CPC upholds the principles of promoting harmony between humanity and nature and selecting officials on the basis of merit. From these I see the connection between China's fine traditional culture and the CPC's governing philosophies, and this helps me better understand the Party's commitment to upholding fundamental principles and breaking new ground. The CPC and the Chinese people are pursing creative transformation and innovative development of traditional Chinese culture on the basis of carrying forward it. In doing so, they develop the Chinese culture and use fine traditional culture to guide China's reform and development.

The principles of acting in good faith, being friendly to others, and fostering neighborliness are reflected in China's diplomacy. China is actively participating in global governance, proposing to the world new ideas and cooperation projects in this field, and providing the international community with more Chinese insight, better Chinese input, and greater Chinese strength.

Now I'd like to elaborate on the concept of building a human community with a shared future and the Belt and Road Initiative; both of them are supported by many countries in the world. They are the crystallization of China's fine traditional culture, and they embody the humanity's shared values and the common interests of the Chinese people and the people around the world. The idea of a community with a shared future is consistent with many concepts in the traditional Chinese culture, such as harmony, coexistence, and peace among all nations. The Belt and Road Initiative is a vivid example of China's efforts to build a human community with a shared future. From the ancient Silk Road and the Belt and Road in the new era, we can see that China remains committed to pursuing mutual benefit and win-win cooperation with other countries, and by advocating the Belt and Road Initiative, China has made important contributions to the world's lasting peace and common prosperity.

In translating the report to the 20th CPC National Congress, I find it both important and challenging to convey the essence of traditional Chinese culture to Russian readers. My colleagues and I worked to first understand the original meaning of these maxims and their connotations in the report, and to make them readable so that Russian readers can truly understand them. We worked to ensure our translation can serve as a bridge that links ancient China and the China today and that links China and the rest of the world. China's fine traditional culture, a valuable asset to the Chinese people, is also exerting a profound influence on the whole world.

The 20th CPC National Congress: Culture and Development

Dragana Mitrovic

Director of Institute of Asian Studies of Political Science
Department, University of Belgrade

The People's Republic of China, built on one of the oldest world civilizations, is in every aspect representative of Chinese culture. The same goes for every Chinese citizen; from the daily life of families and local communities, different levels of government code of conduct, to business circles, products, design, language, cuisine and habits, values and traditions as part of that unique culture are deeply laid. It is the source of self-assurance and confidence, as well as pride in past and recent achievements.

Chinese developmental model is deeply rooted in its culture and tradition.

The developmental strategy presented at the 20th CPC National Congress largely relied on Chinese culture and its long traditions. The CPC's approach to development is the pledge to achieve "high-quality Development" that is "people-centred" and aims to provide "common development." It is rooted in ancient values of solidarity and care for the whole community.

Achieving the goal of eradicating absolute poverty was fulfilling the ancient dream but part of the modern-day Chinese Dream. China managed to fulfil such a magnificent goal after succeeding in elevating hundreds of millions of its citizens from poverty during the process of reform and opening up. Long-term orientation towards high goals is another example of the deep cultural roots of the developmental strategies implemented during "Chinese modernization" and simultaneous urbanization.

"Common development" is exactly the approach the PRC is offering to its partners worldwide through "public goods" and platforms for cooperation, such as the BRI. Oriented towards opening and better-quality connectivity, China is engaged in building a new global development governance and multipolarity where its culture of seeking harmony and peace is at its essence. Traditional Chinese culture respects other cultures because it relies on the Confucian concept of creating a multicultural world through kindness and love. On the other hand, Chinese traditional culture allows harmony that comes from differences that together create the necessary balance. Such an approach creates space for cultural differences and does not seek to impose its views on others. It means that China will impose its cultural and general influence through morality and common achievements rather than through conflicts. At the same time, it is a call for dialogue and mutual engagement with global partners in creating a new multipolar world that would offer developmental chances for all participants.